Investigating Mapwork

Oxford

Investigating Mapwork

Richard Kemp

Oxford University Press 1989

Oxford University Press, Walton Street, Oxford OX2 6DP

Oxford New York Toronto
Delhi Bombay Calcutta Madras Karachi
Petaling Jaya Singapore Hong Kong Tokyo
Nairobi Dar es Salaam Cape Town
Melbourne Auckland

and associated companies in
Berlin Ibadan

Oxford is a trademark of Oxford University Press

© Oxford University Press 1989

ISBN 0 19 913341 7

Typesetting by Burns and Smith, Derby

Printed in Hong Kong

Acknowledgements

The publishers and author would like to thank the following people for their permission to use copyright material.

Photographs

Adkins Photography, **p.24**; Aerofilms, **p.12**, **p.14** (all); British Airways, **p.26**; Richard Kemp, **p.28**; Rod Leach, **p.21**; Archie Miles, **p.33**; OUP, **p.16** (all), **p.25** (all), **p.45** (all); Picturepoint, **p.20**; Scottish Tourist Board / Paul Tomkins, **p.41**; Simon Warner, **p.8** (top and bottom), **p.9**, **p.37**.

Front cover credited to Sealand Aerial Photography.

Illustrations

Terry McKivragen, **p.13**, **p.33** (bottom), **p.37** (bottom).

Maps and diagrams

The map extracts on pages **7**, **11**, **15**, **18**, **19** (six small street maps), **20**, **23**, **31**, **35** (top two), **36**, **39**, **40** (small contoured map), and **43** are reproduced from the Ordnance Survey map, with the permission of Her Majesty's Stationery Office; Crown copyright reserved.

Additional maps and diagrams by Oxford Illustrators Limited.

Contents

1   ASSIGNMENT 1: **North Yorkshire**
MAPSKILLS: Map location   6
INVESTIGATION: Analysing shopping patterns   8

2   ASSIGNMENT 2: **Devon**
MAPSKILLS: Using scales to measure distance   10
INVESTIGATION: A holiday village for Rame Head?   12

3   ASSIGNMENT 3: **Essex**
MAPSKILLS: Aerial photo analysis   14
INVESTIGATION: A new town for Essex?   16

4   ASSIGNMENT 4: **Derbyshire**
MAPSKILLS: Interpreting urban land-use   18
INVESTIGATION: Planning a Geographical Enquiry   21

5   ASSIGNMENT 5: **Glamorgan**
MAPSKILLS: Interpreting industrial land-use   22
INVESTIGATION: Siting a new supermarket   24

6   ASSIGNMENT 6: **Buckinghamshire**
MAPSKILLS: Flows and movements   26
INVESTIGATION: Traffic flows in Aylesbury   28

7   ASSIGNMENT 7: **Gloucestershire**
MAPSKILLS: Interpreting the rural landscape   30
INVESTIGATION: A leisure park for Lechlade?   32

8   ASSIGNMENT 8: **Cumbria**
MAPSKILLS: Contours and relief   34
INVESTIGATION: Siting a new leisure holiday complex   37

9   ASSIGNMENT 9: **Tayside**
MAPSKILLS: Drawing cross-sections   38
INVESTIGATION: Planning a new ski-centre in Glenshee   40

10   ASSIGNMENT 10: **Oxfordshire**
MAPSKILLS: Calculating area   42
INVESTIGATION: Planning a motorway route   44

Legend for 1:50 000 maps   46
Legend for 1:25 000 maps   47

1 MAPSKILLS

ASSIGNMENT 1: North Yorkshire
Map location

Locating something quickly and accurately on a map is a useful skill – directions like 'I think it's somewhere in the middle' are not much use. Two particular skills help you to locate things on a map:
- Using **grid references**
- Using **compass directions**

You may have learnt these two skills already. If so, the ideas and Test Your Skill questions on this page will be revision for you.

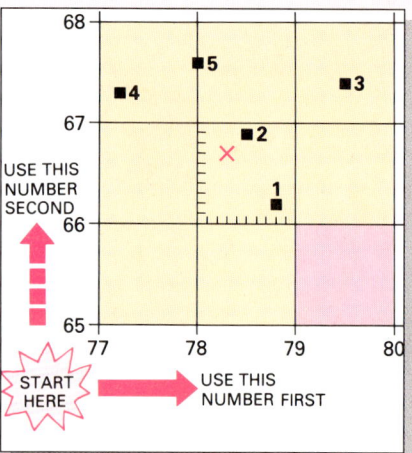

Four figure grid references
The map on the opposite page is covered by equally spaced lines going across and up and down the map. Each line is numbered. The lines form a **grid** of squares. You can use the **map grid** to locate something accurately on the map.

Say you want to locate one particular square – the one shaded red in the diagram, above right.
- Look along the bottom first – the square is numbered **79**.
- Now look up the side – the square is numbered **65**.
- Combine the two numbers to give a **square reference** of **7965**.
  Notice that we do not put any space between the numbers when they are combined.

Six figure grid references
If you want to locate a point *inside* one of the grid squares, you have to use a **six figure reference**. Say you want to give the exact location of the red cross inside square 7866.
- To make your job easier notice that the sides of the square have been divided into 10 equal parts.
- Normally you would have to imagine this for yourself.
- Look along the bottom first – the cross is 3 parts along, so **783**.
- Now look up the side – the cross is 7 parts up, so **667**.
- Combine the two numbers to give a six figure grid reference of **783667**.

Remember!
- Always start from the lower left hand corner
- Always look at the bottom line number first
- Don't leave any spaces when you combine the numbers

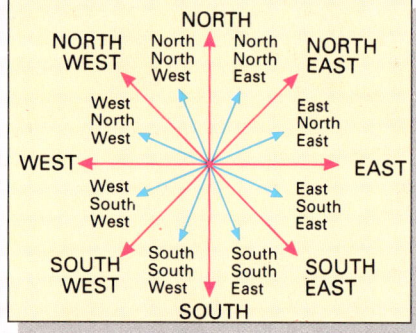

Test your skill 1
Grid references and compass directions

1. Using the diagram above, work out the six figure grid references for each of the black squares numbered 1–5.

2. Using the map on the opposite page. What are the four figure references of these villages?
   a Austwick   b Clapham   c Lawkland

3. What is the compass direction from:
   a Austwick to Horton-in-Ribblesdale?
   b Settle to Clapham?
   c Stainforth to Austwick?
   d Horton-in-Ribblesdale to Stainforth?

4. How many churches with towers are there in the area shown by the map? Work out the six figure grid references of each of them.

5. What would you find actually on the ground at each of these map references? Check with the symbols key on page 46 if you need to.
   a 775665   b 732678   c 812695   d 808723
   e 799644

Test your skill 2
Settlements

The map on the opposite page shows part of the district around the market town of Settle in North Yorkshire.

1. a What evidence is there on the map to show that Clapham (7469) has many visitors during the year?
   b What evidence is there to explain why some people come here?
   c Looking at the area as a whole, what other facilities and services are there that visitors might use?

2. a What do you notice about the location of settlements in relation to the height of the land? (To help you answer this question the map shows all the land over the height of 250m in solid brown.)

3. All the larger settlements are located on or near the more important roads. Which do you think came first – the places or the roads? Give the reasons for your answer.

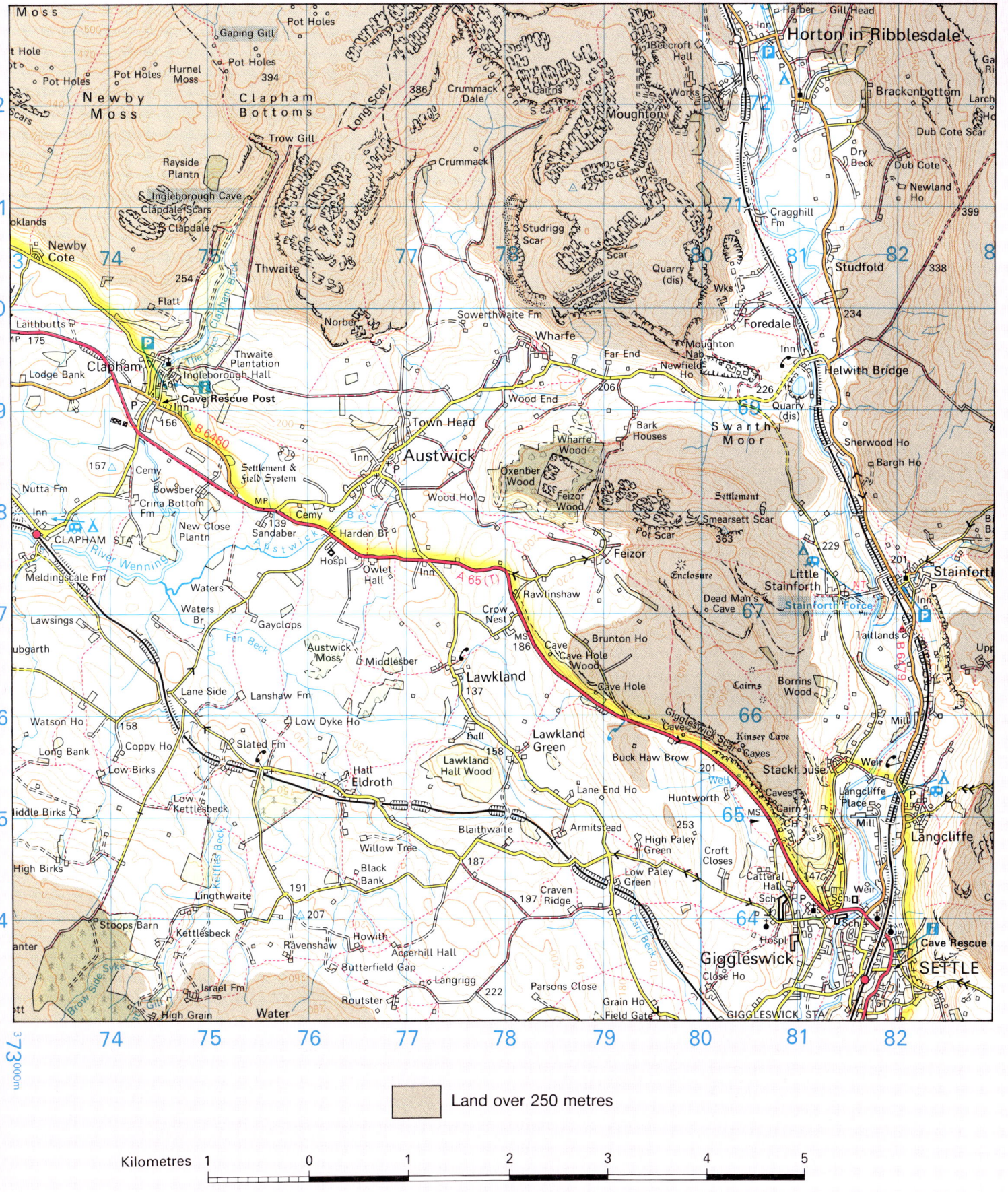

INVESTIGATION 1

Analysing shopping patterns
North Yorkshire

Briefing

With the exception of the small market town of Settle, all the settlements shown on the map on the previous page are small, fairly isolated rural villages.

A fieldwork survey was carried out in two of the villages, **Austwick** and **Horton-in-Ribblesdale**, to find out the shopping patterns of people living in the villages.

Your task is to use the fieldwork data to map and analyse the results of the survey.

Work on your own to complete both work programmes.

Report Back
Your finished work should include 3 maps and some written answers.

Services and facilities	Austwick	Horton
Post Office	✓	
Call box	✓	✓
Village shop	✓	✓
Pub	✓	✓
Church/chapel	✓	✓
Primary school	✓	
Garage	✓	
Bus service	✓	✓

Austwick village centre

Work programme A
Mapping the shopping patterns

The base map on the opposite page shows the towns that are closest to the two villages – the larger the circle the larger the town.

- On your own copy of the base map (or on a tracing overlay), make a map to show shopping movements from **Austwick** for
  a Christmas shopping   b shopping for shoes
- Draw one line from Austwick to show the shopping movement of each person. Use different colours for the two different types of shopping.
- Use another base map to draw a map showing the same information for people from **Horton-in-Ribblesdale**.
- Using the map on the previous page, make your own map which shows the food shopping movements of people from both villages. It is up to you to decide on the best way of mapping this data.

Horton, the village store

Work programme B
Analysing the patterns

Look at your two maps of Christmas and shoes shopping. Describe, and compare, the patterns that the two maps show;

- How do the Christmas and shoes shopping patterns differ? What might be the reasons for this?
- In what ways are the patterns on the two maps similar or different? What might explain the differences?
- Why do you suppose that some people are prepared to travel all the way to Bradford and Leeds, when there are other large places closer by?
- According to the information from this survey nobody shops in some of the towns shown on the base map. What reasons do you think there are to explain this situation?

Describe the pattern that your food shopping map shows.

- How are the patterns for the two villages similar or different? What might help to account for the differences?

Fieldwork data (Sample of 25 people asked from each village)

'What is the main place you go to for your Christmas shopping?'

	in village	Settle	Lancaster	Skipton	Keighley	Bradford	Leeds
Austwick	–	1	7	4	1	5	7
Horton	–	3	–	5	4	6	7

'Where do you most often go to shop for shoes?'

	in village	Settle	Lancaster	Skipton	Keighley	Bradford	Leeds
Austwick	–	7	4	9	1	1	3
Horton	–	10	–	11	1	–	3

'Where do you go most often to do your main food shopping?'

	in village	Settle	Lancaster	Skipton	Keighley	Bradford	Leeds
Austwick	9	14	–	2	–	–	–
Horton	4	18	–	3	–	–	–

Settle market place

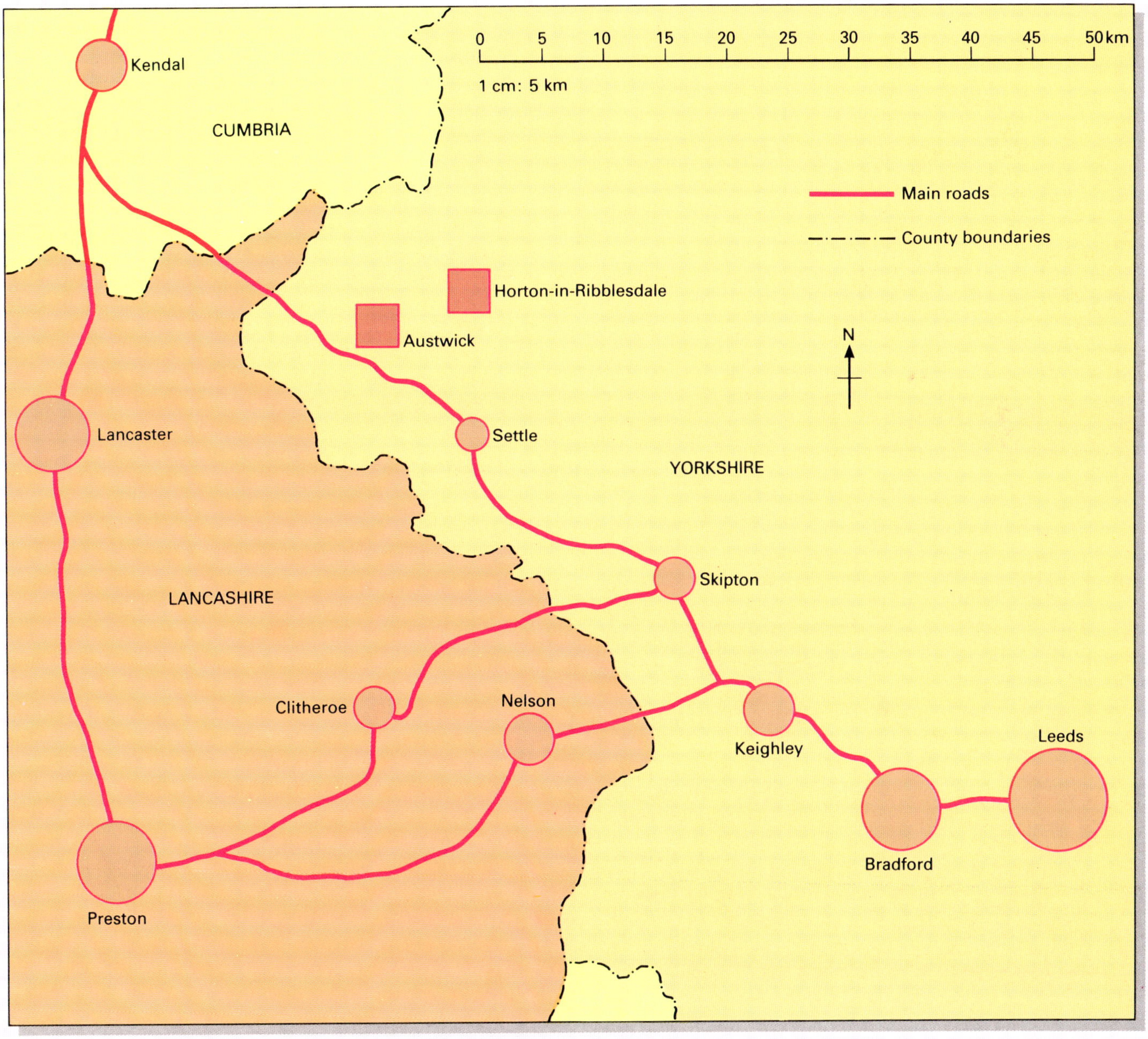

9

2 MAPSKILLS

ASSIGNMENT 2: Devon
Using scales to measure distance

One of the main uses of all sorts of maps is to work out the distances between places. We can do this accurately because maps have been carefully drawn **to scale**.

In the same way that a model ship or car is a scaled down version of the real thing, so a map is a scaled down representation of what is found on the ground. To use a map to work out actual distances on the ground we have to use the **scale** of that particular map.

Types of scales

- **Line (or linear) scale:** There is a line scale below the map on the opposite page.
- **Written scale:** If you measure the divisions on the line scale opposite you will find that each part of the line scale is 2cm long. Each 2cm of the scale represents 1km actually on the ground. So another way of giving this scale is to write **2cm:1km**.
- **Representative fraction:** This scale can be shown in another way. Each 1cm on the map represents 50 000cm on the actual ground – this is how much the map has scaled down what is on the ground, so this can be shown as **1:50 000**.

Measuring straightline and non-direct distances

The upper coloured box on the right explains how to measure straightline, or direct, distances. In this case you are working out the actual direct distance between points A and B on a map.

But let's say that there is a road between two places on a map, and you want to measure the distance you would actually have to travel along the road. This actual distance will, of course, be slightly longer than the direct distance. The way of measuring non-direct distances is explained in the lower coloured box on this page.

Measuring straightline distances

1 Using the edge of a piece of paper, or a ruler, measure the distance on the map

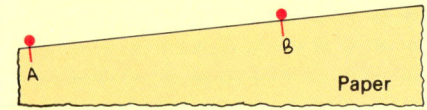

2 Place the paper along the scale, making sure the first mark is by the 0 on the scale. Read off the distance – in this example, it is 3·4 km.

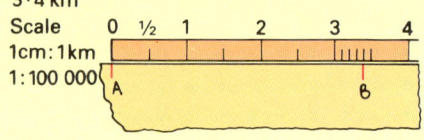

Measuring non-direct distances

Say you want to measure the distance along the road between the two churches:

1 Place one corner of a piece of paper by West Church, with edge of the paper lined up along the road. At the first corner in the road, make a mark on the paper.

2 Keeping your first mark on the same point, rotate the paper, so that the edge is now lined up along the next section of road. Make a second mark at the second corner in the road.

3 Keeping your second mark on the same point, rotate the paper again so that the edge is now lined up along the next section of road. Make a third mark at the next corner.

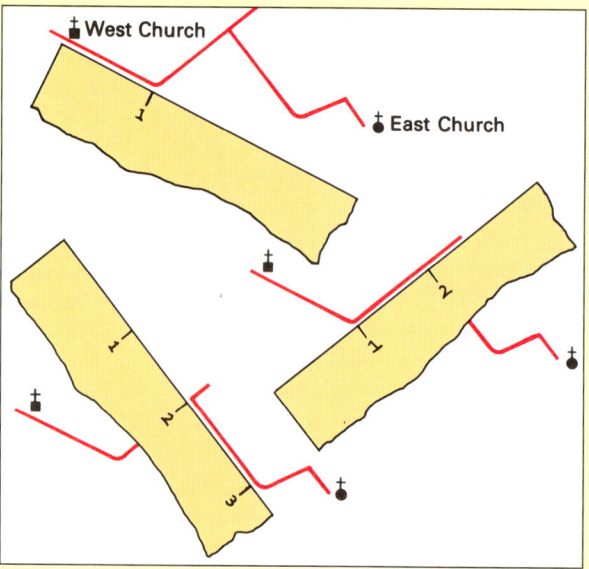

4 Carry on marking and turning the paper until you reach East Church. The length of paper between the corner of the paper and your last mark is the actual road distance between the two churches. Measure this length against the scale, and it will give the road distance in kilometres.

Test your skill 1
Measuring distances

1 Work out the direct, or straightline distance between these pairs of places on the OS map opposite. Write your answers in kilometres.
  a The churches at 446520 and 463550.
  b The main railway station (477553) and the station in square 4556.

2 If you had to travel along the main roads from the main railway station to the station in square 4556, how many kilometres would the journey be?

3 Your boat is moored at Wearde Quay (4257). You plan to sail from there to Pier Cellars (4449). If you keep roughly to the centre of the channel, work out the distance you would have to sail.

4 You want to travel from Rame Church (4249) to the Information Centre in Plymouth (4755)
  a What is the direct distance between the two places?
  b Work out the shortest route if you go by car. Measure the road distance you would have to travel. You will need to use a ferry – be sure to use a ferry that carries vehicles (V).
  c What is the shortest distance if you wanted to walk? Again you will need to use a ferry – it could be a ferry that only carries passengers (P).

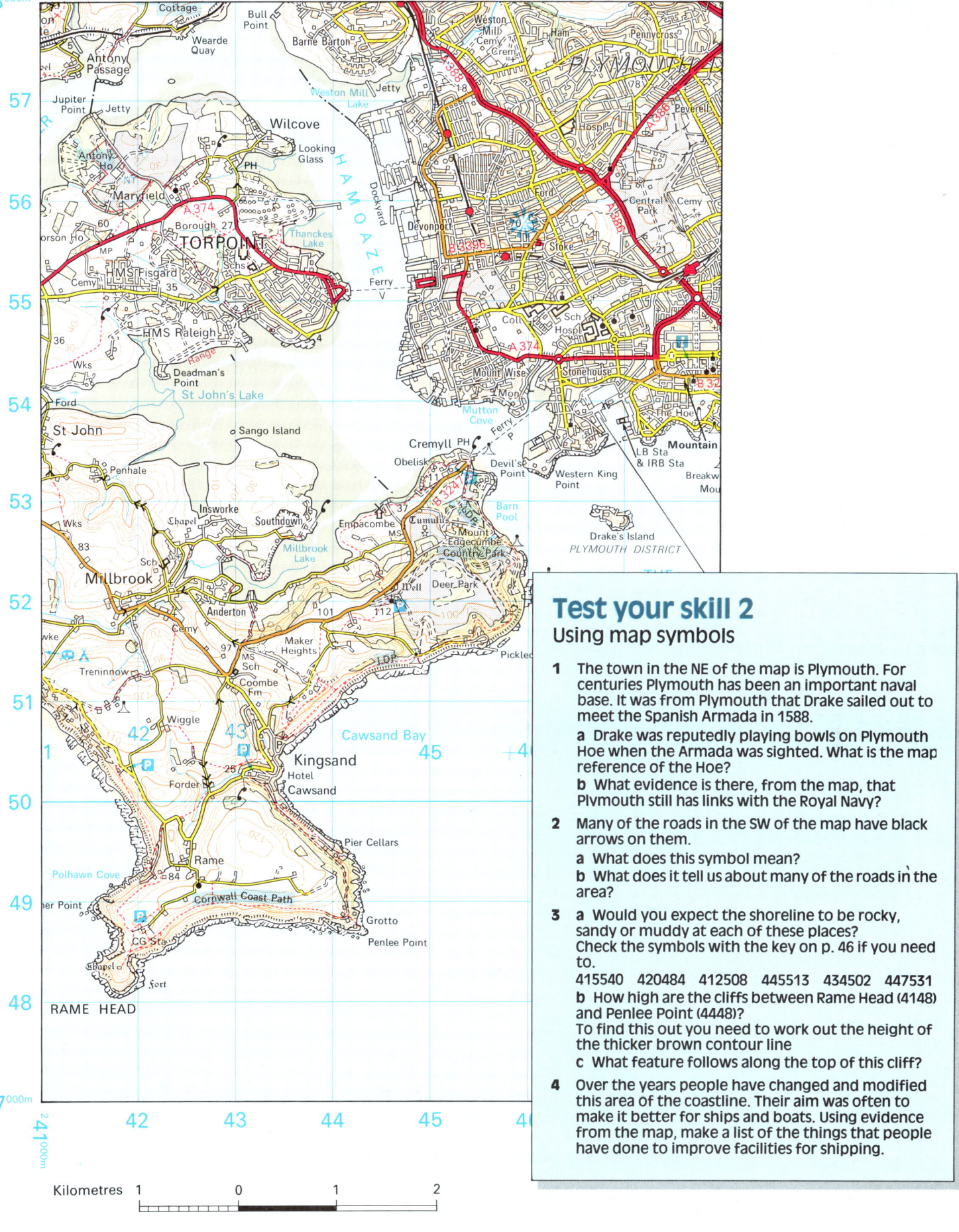

Test your skill 2
Using map symbols

1 The town in the NE of the map is Plymouth. For centuries Plymouth has been an important naval base. It was from Plymouth that Drake sailed out to meet the Spanish Armada in 1588.

  a Drake was reputedly playing bowls on Plymouth Hoe when the Armada was sighted. What is the map reference of the Hoe?

  b What evidence is there, from the map, that Plymouth still has links with the Royal Navy?

2 Many of the roads in the SW of the map have black arrows on them.

  a What does this symbol mean?

  b What does it tell us about many of the roads in the area?

3 a Would you expect the shoreline to be rocky, sandy or muddy at each of these places?
Check the symbols with the key on p. 46 if you need to.
415540 420484 412508 445513 434502 447531

  b How high are the cliffs between Rame Head (4148) and Penlee Point (4448)?
To find this out you need to work out the height of the thicker brown contour line

  c What feature follows along the top of this cliff?

4 Over the years people have changed and modified this area of the coastline. Their aim was often to make it better for ships and boats. Using evidence from the map, make a list of the things that people have done to improve facilities for shipping.

INVESTIGATION 2

Devon
A holiday village for Rame Head?

Briefing

A London-based leisure and building consortium would like to develop a holiday village complex on a site at Rame in Cornwall. Rame is located in Square 4249 on the map on the previous page.

The planned development would be for 18 holiday chalets, and shop and leisure facilities. The brochure gives an idea of the development. The photo includes the proposed site of the development.

Your task in this investigation is to consider what the effects might be on the local area if this development went ahead.

Working in a pair or small group, it is up to you to decide on the most effective way of completing all the work programmes. Some ideas on how to report back are outlined in the work programmes.

Rame Head

Work programmes A and B

A: Locating the planned development

Draw a large sketch map of the Rame Head area with the planned development clearly indicated.

B: What might be the views of local people?

What do you think these people or groups might feel about the planned development of the holiday village?

- owner of a weekend cottage in Rame
- owner of the shop/post office in Kingsand
- local farmer's union
- local environmental protection group
- person who runs a taxi service based in Millbrook

Report back
Decide how you want to present these viewpoints
- as taped or written interviews
- as letters to the local press
- in some other form that you think would be effective

Work programme C
What might be the impact on the local environment?

A new development such as this will have an impact on the local area. What do you think the impact is likely to be on:
- the landscape of the local area?
- the pattern of local employment?
- the local road and transport situation?
- the general amenities of the locality?

Report back
Write or tape a short report on the possible impact. Use the four headings you have been given, but add more headings if you think they are important.

MAPSKILLS 3

ASSIGNMENT 3: Essex
Aerial photo analysis

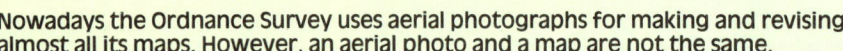

Nowadays the Ordnance Survey uses aerial photographs for making and revising almost all its maps. However, an aerial photo and a map are not the same.

An **aerial photo** is a snapshot of everything the camera sees at one particular point in time. Some of that information will be useful, but some of it may be confusing or difficult to interpret.

A **map** *selects* and *emphasises* things that are likely to be useful to the people who will be using the map. It can also include *additional information* that cannot be shown on the photo. The map does this by using *symbols, standard colours, names* and *numbers*.

Vertical and oblique views

In taking an aerial photo the camera can either be pointing directly downwards (a *vertical* view), or sideways-and-downwards (an *oblique* view). The two small aerial photos are vertical and oblique views of the same area. Look at them carefully and notice the differences between the two photos.

When analysing and interpreting aerial photos you need to take account of:
- shape and size
- shades and colours
- shadows
- patterns
- textures

Test your skill 1 Using a black and white aerial photo

All these questions are linked to the aerial photo above. Remember to **explain** your answers fully, by using **evidence** located on the photo.

1. Is this a vertical or oblique view photo?
2. Was the photo taken in winter or summer? (*Look at the vegetation*)
3. At about what time was the photo taken – early morning, midday or late evening? (*Look at the shadow*)
4. What are the buildings in square E1 used for? (*Look at the pattern and shape*)
5. Is the farmland in squares B3 and D1 used for grassland or cereal crops? (*Look at the texture and patterns on the photo*)
6. Is the road in E2 single or dual carriage?
7. How is the land being used in square C2?
8. Is the building marked 'A' old or new? What evidence is there to support your answer?

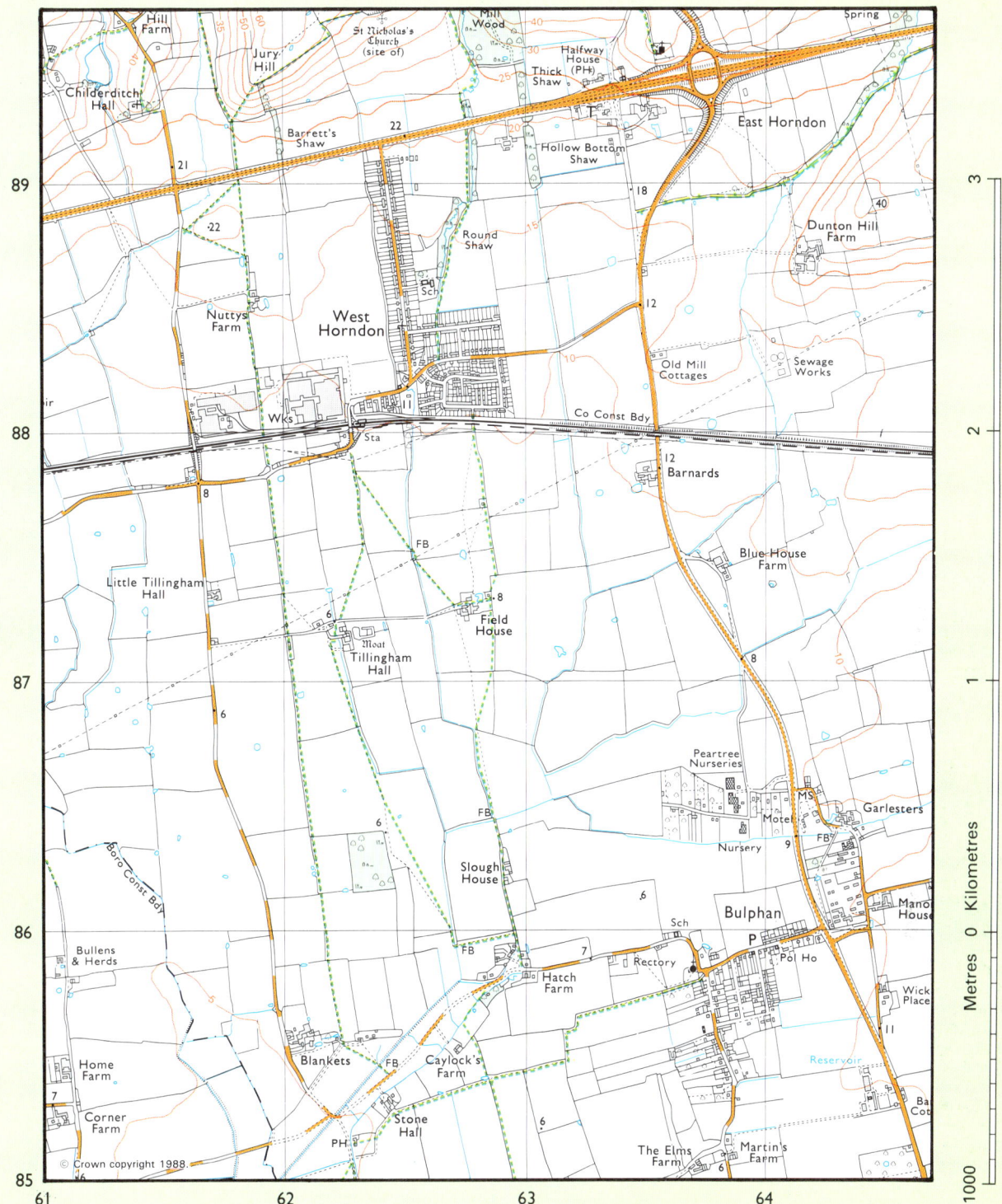

Test your skill 2 — Using a map and aerial photo together

The photo on the opposite page shows part of the area covered by the OS 1:25 000 map above. The questions ask you to link map and photo information.

1. Is the settlement shown in photo squares C2 & D2 called **Bulphan** or **West Horndon**?

2. a Give the 4-figure map reference of the farm at the top of photo square A2.
   b Give the name and 6-figure map reference of the building marked A.

3. Using the information from your answers to questions 1 & 2, say in which direction the camera was pointing when the photo was taken.

4. What is the name of:
   a the house at the top of photo square A3?
   b the farms in photo square C1?

5. Work out which map squares are covered completely or partly by the aerial photo. Draw a simple sketch map to show this information.

6. Compare the area that is covered by both the map and the aerial photo.
   a what information does the map provide that cannot be discovered by just using the photo?
   b what information does the photo provide that the map does not?

3 INVESTIGATION

A new town for Essex?

Briefing

The area around Tillingham Hall in Essex recently became a centre of controversy: the newspaper article, and the other information on these pages, helps to explain why.

On any major planning issue like this different people have differing views about what should happen. Your task is to examine the Tillingham Hall New Town proposal, and consider some of those different viewpoints.

First private new town in 100 years planned

PLANS for Britain's first private new town in almost 100 years, swallowing 760 acres of prime Green Belt land in South Essex, were unveiled on Tuesday.

The town provisionally named Tillingham Hall, would house 15,000 people in 5,000 homes, and would include four schools, light and high tech industry, a health centre, church, multi-purpose community halls and high street grouped around an artificial lake and surrounded by parkland.

Consortium Developments Ltd. formed in 1983 by nine private housebuilders including Wimpey, Bovis Homes and Barratt Developments, submitted an outline planning application to Thurrock Council on Wednesday.

Tuesday's unveiling at Bulphan's Plough Motel met with a hostile reception from several hundred protestors from West Horndon, Bulphan and Thurrock.

Announcing the plan, Consortium Developments' executive director, Mr Andy Bennett, said: "The plan for new county towns is an imaginative and practical private sector initiative to tackle the region's increasingly difficult housing problem.

"By the end of this decade many hopeful home-owners especially first-time buyers, are going to be priced out of the market," he said. "Inevitably this means releasing more land for housing than is currently planned and this raised the whole conservation issue. We hope to be able to carry out our proposals in close co-operation with the relevant authorities."

Brentwood Council's chief executive, Mr Colin Sivell who attended the meeting with the council's director of planning, Mr Russel Davies, protested that Brentwood had not been consulted.

"We were given a copy of a hazy plan carrying very little detail," he said. "If public consultation is to mean anything I must insist that my council receives full documentation," said Mr Sivell.

Later he said: "I am astonished by the cavalier way in which public consultation on this very important issue has been conducted."

Warley councillor Mr Alan Earl said: "This plan drives a coach and horses through the Green Belt policy" and chairman of Brentwood Council David Ramsey commented: "This plan offers no gains for the community at large and, apart from anything else, will intensify the already appalling traffic density on the A127."

Essex County Councillor Mr Michael Bidmead said: "There will be enough land available to meet housing needs of the county."

Essex County Council's planning committee chairman Robert Daniels said this week: "All parties at County Hall are united in opposition to any encroachment into the Green Belt."

The opposition to the plan will probably mean a public enquiry, with the final decision being taken by Environment Secretary Patrick Jenkin.

Plans will be on public display at West Horndon village hall next Wednesday and Mr Stephen Stone, chairman of West Horndon Residents' Association said: "I am completely overawed at the extent of these proposals and very concerned that they might be eventually extended north of the village as well."

Mr Philip Warner, chief executive of Bovis Homes who chaired Tuesday's unveiling, confirmed that two farmers had already signed over their properties to the consortium. "They will be selling their land if we gain planning consent. But I am not prepared to reveal their names," he said.

'I don't know that much about it really, but from what I know the plan doesn't bother me. If farmers want to sell their land at a decent profit, that's their business. A few more houses isn't going to make that much difference around here. Anyway, industry and commerce desperately needs land to expand around London. Successful businesses provide jobs. Jobs mean people, and people need somewhere nice to live.'

LOCAL RESIDENT

'There are 250 000 people in London who need houses, but so far they have no voice. We are going to invest almost £500 million at Tillingham Hall, building homes and services that are badly needed in the South East around London. How else will young people be able to afford homes?'

SPOKESPERSON CONSORTIUM DEVELOPMENTS LTD

'A new town on our doorstep would swamp us and eventually destroy us. If we wanted to live in a new town we could move to one – what we don't want is a new town to move in on us. Besides, 15 000 people mean up to 7 500 more cars. The local roads are overcrowded already, any more cars and lorries will make the situation intolerable, and very dangerous'

WEST HORNDON RESIDENT

'We haven't been given enough information. The developers have provided fancy drawings to show how nice it would be – a lake and all that. But we can't decide until we have the full facts. Who is going to pay for the running of the services in the new town? If it provides new jobs for local people I might support the idea, but local people deserve to have more information.'

LOCAL COUNCILLOR

'This is Green Belt land. We must protect these open spaces on the edge of London. There is so much pressure on it all the time. Any money spent here in the Green Belt won't be spent where it is needed most – in the decaying inner city areas of London, where people really need homes.'

COUNCIL FOR THE PROTECTION OF RURAL ENGLAND

Work programmes A–E

Work in a pair or small group to complete all the tasks. First, everyone in your group needs to read through all the information provided.

Then, as a group, discuss the issue, and decide how you are going to work to tackle the tasks most effectively.

Report back
As a group present your work in a Report folder. Make sure it has a proper title and contents list.

A: What is the plan?
- What is being proposed for the 760 acre site at Tillingham Hall?
- Who wants to develop this site?
- What details are there about the plan?
- What do the developers say are the advantages of the plan?

B: Where might it all happen?
The site of the proposed new town is shown on the map on the previous page. In the box (below, right) are grid reference directions which tell you where the site boundaries are.
- Place a sheet of tracing paper over the OS map, and work out exactly where the site is located
- On your tracing add any other map information that you think is important in this whole issue.

C: What are local peoples' reactions?
- Many of the local objectors said that the plan went against the Green Belt regulations.
What is the Green Belt, and why is the Green Belt an important point when thinking about this new town proposal?
- What seemed to be the main objections of the local councils?
- What were the reasons for many local resident's objections?

D: Organising public meetings
One of the difficulties of the Tillingham Hall plan is that many people feel that they do not have the full facts.
One answer to this is to organise public meetings, at which people can be given information and have the chance to ask questions.

Design an effective poster to publicise each of these two public meetings that are being organised. Each poster should be no larger than a single sheet of normal file paper.
- A meeting in the village hall organised by the Bulphan Villagers' Protest Group
- A publicity meeting organised by Consortium Developments Ltd, to take place in Bulphan village hall.

E: Writing to the press
In an issue like this the local press plays an important part. Articles inform people of developments, and people can write to the press to express their views.
Write two fairly short, but hard-hitting, letters to the Essex Gazette. Both are from local people – one who is mainly for the plan, and one who is mainly against the plan.

The London Green Belt is a ring of land around the capital which is protected from further housing and industrial development.

London is one of a number of cities in Britain which have a green belt. Local councils and conservation organisations argue that the Green Belt is a vital protection against large-scale development, which could cause the suburbs of London to sprawl out to join surrounding towns.

Developers argue that there is so much demand for new housing and industrial development in the crowded South East around London, that they should be allowed to build in a number of selected places. Only this will allow the demand for houses to be met.

THE ESSEX GREEN BELT

These directions will allow you to trace around the proposed Tillingham Hall New Town site

1. Follow the minor road north from 618864 to 617878 (but not including Little Tillingham Hall)
2. Follow the minor road from 617878 as far as the railway at 623880
3. Along the south side of the railway from 623880 to the road at 635879
4. Follow the road south from 635879 to 639871 (but not including Barnards)
5. Follow the track south from 639871 to the corner of Peartree Nurseries at 639867
6. Follow the field boundaries and ditch west from 639867 to 627864
7. From 627864 follow around the field boundary to the eastern edge of the wood at 625863
8. Follow around the wood, which is included in the planned site to 623864
9. From 623864 follow the field boundaries across to the road at 618864

You should now be back where you started!
Everywhere inside your line is part of the proposed new town site.

4 MAPSKILLS

ASSIGNMENT 4: Derbyshire
Interpreting urban land-use

It is in towns and cities that people make the most concentrated use of the land we live on. The amount of urban land-use detail that can be shown on a map depends mainly on the scale of the map. The larger the scale of the map, the more detailed the information can be. These are just some questions we can try and answer by looking at a map of a town.

- What are these buildings **used** for?
- **What sort** of houses are these?
- Where is the **oldest** part of the town?
- Where is the main **shopping centre**?
- How has the town **grown**?

OS maps mainly provide **clues** rather than much factual information about urban land-use. We have to use those clues to give us the **evidence** to try and answer questions like the ones on the left.

What sort of clues can we look for?

- **names**, **abbreviations** and **symbols**
- the **size** and **shape** of buildings
- the **spacing** of buildings
- the **pattern** of buildings and roads
- the **situation** of buildings within the town

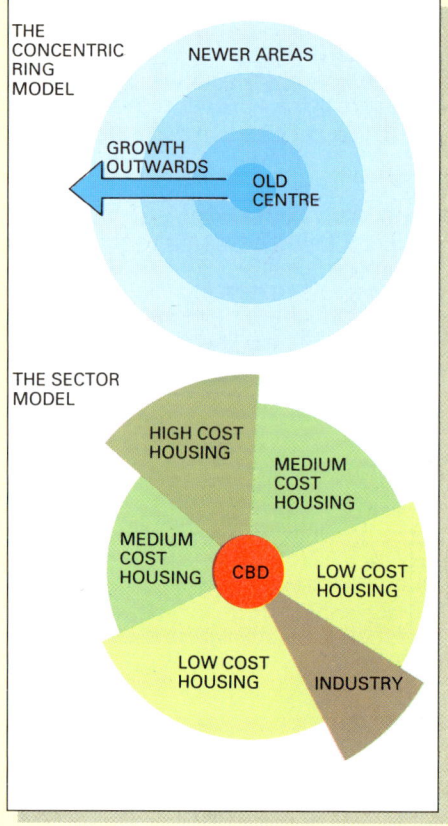

Patterns of town growth

The oldest part of the town is usually the *town centre* (although over the years many of the buildings will have been rebuilt). The town centre is usually the main shopping and business area, and is called the *central business district* or CBD.

Most towns have grown outwards from the old centre, in rings of growth, as the *concentric ring model* shows. Few towns are completely round though, and growth may be concentrated along main transport routes.

The *sector model* shows how, in many towns, different types of land-use often concentrate in different parts of the town. The CBD is one example. Other land-uses form sectors. We would expect to find the older housing in a sector nearer the old centre, and newer housing nearer the edge of town.

To identify the town centre look out for:
- the pattern of roads converging (coming together)
- small, older streets, closely spaced
- a concentration of churches
- a concentration of public buildings, such as the Town Hall and tourist information centre
- the railway station is often at the edge of the town centre; the bus station may be in the centre
- don't forget the obvious – the town centre is likely to be fairly central in the town!

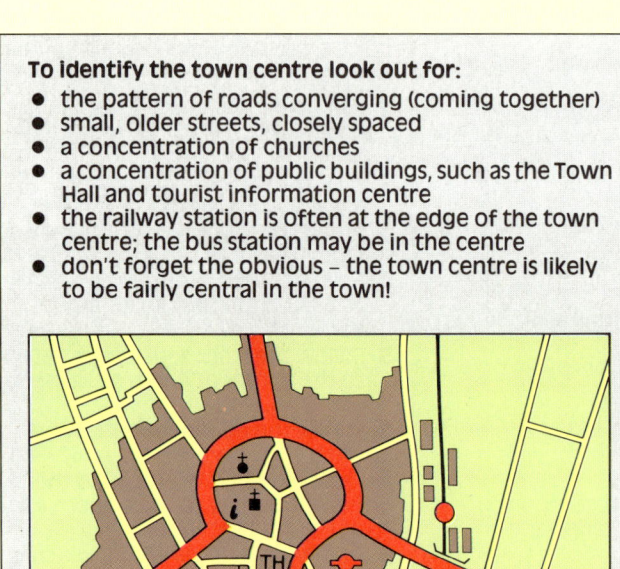

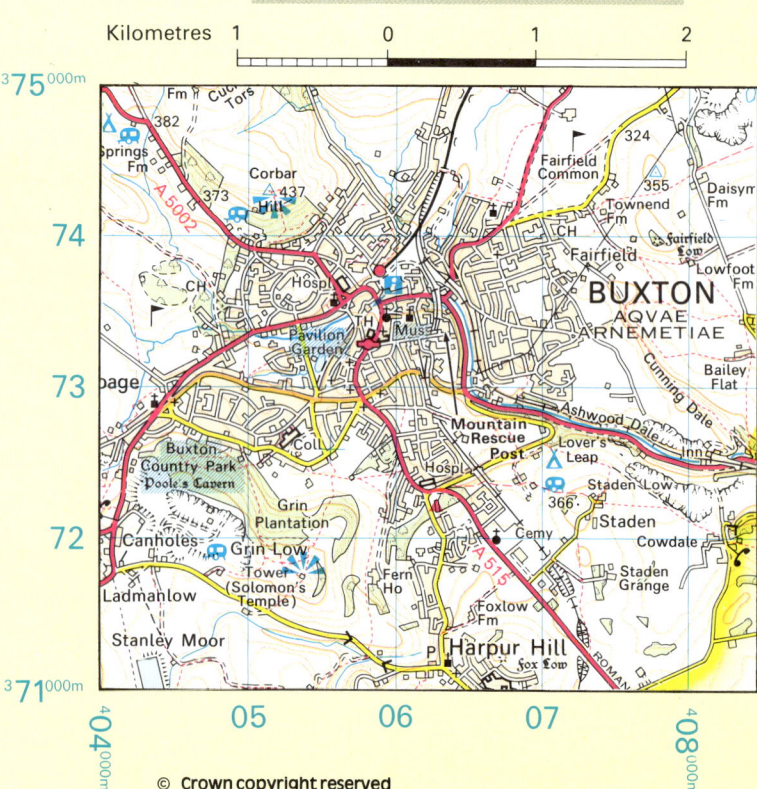

© Crown copyright reserved

18

Patterns of housing

A: Older low cost housing (pre 1914)
- Back to back terraced houses
- Straight, closely spaced streets
- Little or no garden
  Note also: *nearby factory and canal*

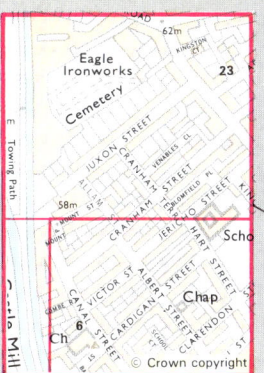

E: Newer high cost housing (post 1945)
- Widely spaced houses, with large gardens
- Planned road pattern

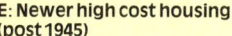

B: Older high cost housing (pre 1914)
- Larger size of buildings
- More widely spaced
- Large gardens
  Note also: *building large enough to convert to hotel*

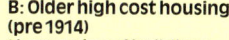

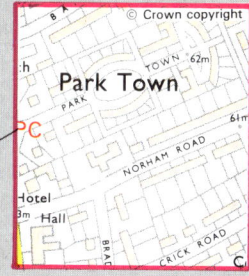

F: Old housing (former outlying village swallowed by growth of town)
- Little regular pattern to houses
- Large and small houses mixed together
  Note also: *the road name*

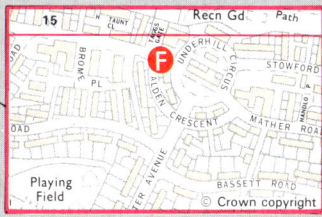

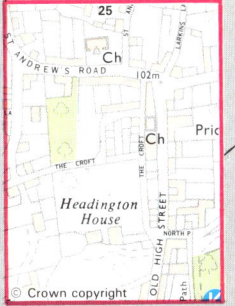

C: Between the wars low cost housing (1920–40)
- Small, closely spaced houses, but with gardens
- Houses in straight rows
  Note also: *nearby school and park*

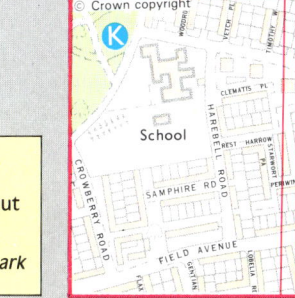

D: Newer low cost housing (post 1945)
- Small closely spaced houses, with gardens
- Curving and circular road patterns
  Note also: *nearby playing field*

Test your skill 1
Map symbols

Use the OS 1:50 000 map on the opposite page, which shows the town of Buxton.

1. How is the land being used at each of these places?
   a 056737 b 053726 c 059738 d 073746

2. a What would be the difference in the appearance of the two buildings at 059735 and 061735?
   b How is the use of the buildings at 062724 and 053726 different?
   c What is the difference between the use of the buildings at 059738 and 058733?

3. a What do the two blue symbols at 052743 mean?
   b Is the lake at Stanley Moor (0471) a natural lake or a manmade reservoir? Explain the evidence you used to come to your answer.

4. In which grid square, or squares, is the centre of Buxton? Explain what evidence you used to give your answer.

5. What map evidence is there that Buxton is:
   a a very old settlement?
   b an important tourist centre?

Test your skill 2
Urban patterns

The OS map on Page 20 also shows Buxton, but at the larger 1:25 000 scale. Use that map to answer these questions.

1. Give the 6 figure reference of the Town Hall.

2. Using evidence from the map, say as much as you can about the type of housing around each of these locations.
   If you need to, check with the **Patterns of Housing** information box on this page.
   a 056727 b 063725 c 055735 d 071731

3. What evidence is there on the map to show that land in Buxton is used for industry?

4. Buxton has not grown as much in a northward direction as it has in other directions. Why do you think this is? Clue: look at the contour lines and shape of the land.

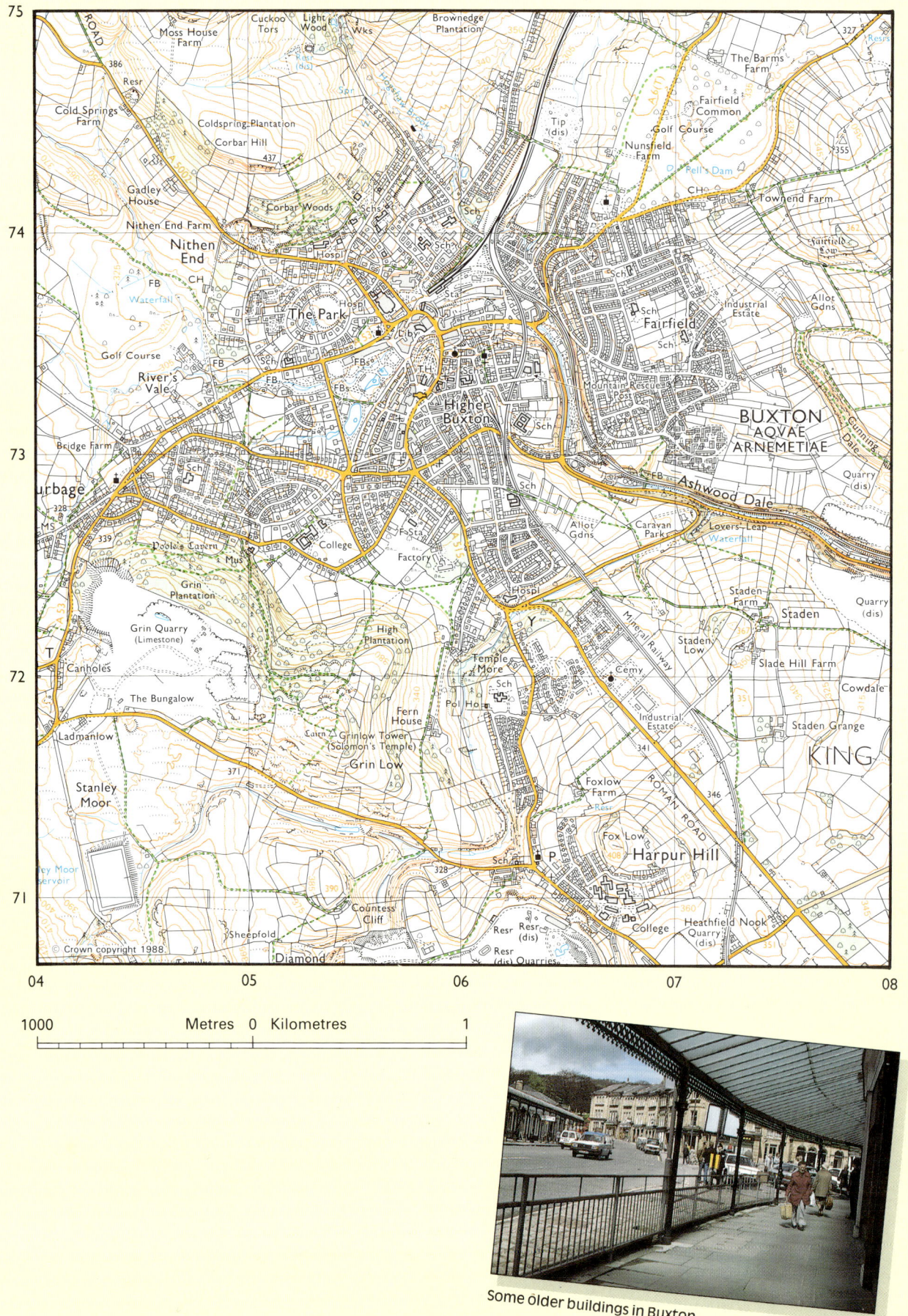

Some older buildings in Buxton

Derbyshire
Planning a Geographical Enquiry

Briefing
You have a day to do some fieldwork in Buxton. Using the map, your task is to plan how you would organise and carry out that fieldwork, as part of a geographical enquiry.

Work programme
Work either on your own, or in a pair.
Here are two possible geographical enquiry titles. For Enquiry A there are detailed planning guidelines below.

Enquiry A: Where is the central business district of Buxton, and how large is it?

Enquiry B: To test the hypothesis that the volume of road traffic will decrease as you move away from town centre

Choose one of these two enquiry titles for your planning work. If you choose Enquiry B you have the opportunity to do the planning from scratch. However, you may find it useful to use the Enquiry A guidelines, as they will give you an idea of what your planning work should involve.

Report back
Produce a written 'Enquiry planning outline'. Where necessary use diagrams and sketch maps to illustrate your planning work.

Buxton, the town centre

Enquiry A: guidelines
Where is the CBD of Buxton, and how large is it?

1 Aims
The aims of this enquiry are to use fieldwork to:
- find the location of the CBD
- work out the area that it covers
- record this information in map form

Write the enquiry title and aims at the top of your *Planning outline*.

2 Background information
The CBD is a zone in the town that is very different from other zones. Three of its characteristics are:
- it has a concentration of particular types of land-use
- its buildings tend to be taller than those in other parts of town
- it has the greatest concentration of pedestrians during the day

In your *Planning outline* describe these characteristics in more detail. For example: what types of land-use are concentrated in the CBD? what types of land-use are **not** found in the CBD?

Using map evidence, say where you think the CBD of Buxton is likely to be.

To collect the data for your enquiry you can concentrate on one of these characteristics. Which one do you think would be the best?

3 Selecting fieldwork methods
How are you going to collect the data needed for this enquiry? Think about the possible methods, and any equipment or resources you might need.

Remember: you have a day to do the fieldwork.

In your *Planning outline* describe:
- what possible methods you considered
- which method, or methods, you selected, and why.

4 Planning the fieldwork
How would you carry out the fieldwork?
This is where you need to make more detailed plans. To do this you need to use the map to plan actual locations.

In your *Planning outline* describe in detail:
- where you would collect data
- how exactly you would collect data
- how would you record the data in the field?
- what possible difficulties might arise?

5 Showing the results
Finally, how would you plan to present the results of the data you collected?
Briefly describe your ideas in your *Planning outline*.

INVESTIGATION 4

MAPSKILLS 5

ASSIGNMENT 5: Glamorgan
Interpreting industrial land-use

OS maps, like the ones in this book, give us only a limited amount of information about industrial land-use.

Service Industry
The majority of working people have jobs in *service industries*, for example in offices and shops. Much of this type of industry cannot show up on OS maps, although there are some clues:
- concentrations of service industry jobs in town and city centres
- public service jobs in hospitals, colleges and schools
- seaside and holiday areas have concentrations of tourist-linked service jobs

Manufacturing Industry
OS maps use words like *works* and *mill* to show large-scale *manufacturing* industry. Maps do not usually say what industry is involved, but it is possible to use map clues to make reasoned guesses, based on:
- the size and arrangement of buildings
- the type of transport links
- the location and surroundings

Primary Industry
Primary industries employ comparatively few people, but they do have an important impact on the environment. OS maps give information and clues about *farming*, *forestry*, *mining* and *quarrying*.

Primary Industry: Mining and Quarrying

Mines (most often coal mines) have *buildings* and often *rail links*. Look for the word '*mine*' and for nearby *waste heaps*.

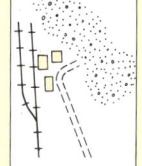

Quarries are where rock is taken from a hillside. Look for the symbol and the word '*quarry*'. Larger quarries have *buildings* for processing, and possibly *rail links*.

Open pits are where sand and gravel are extracted, and are usually located in lowland river valleys. Disused gravel pits may be shown on OS maps as *lakes*.

Manufacturing industry

Large factories usually mean **heavy industry**. Sometimes the type of industry is indicated, but usually not.
Examples could be **metal industries** and **engineering**.

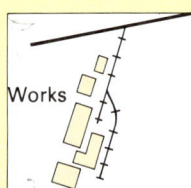

Clues to look for:
1. *Large buildings*
2. The word '*works*' which usually means that it is all part of one large plant
3. *Rail links*, which indicate heavy, bulky materials are moved

Test your skill

Using the information on the 1:50 000 map opposite:

1. What do the industrial or transport symbols at each of these grid references represent?
   a 640985 b 610982 c 670960 d 615003 e 610977

2. Using evidence from the map, say as much as you can about the industrial activity in each of these grid squares:
   a 5901 b 5998 c 6095/6096 d 6692/6792/6791

3. What is manufactured at the factory at 643000? What else does the map tell us about the way this factory operates?

4. What map evidence is there that there have been **changes** in:
   a the mining industry in this area?
   b the use of the docks?

Port locations attract some industries which import large amounts of raw material.
Oil refining and **chemical works** are two examples.

Clues to look for:
1. The words '*docks*' and '*jetties*'
2. *Round storage tanks* for oil and chemicals
3. *Rail links* to move refined products

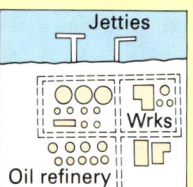

Industrial estates are often identified on OS maps, sometimes using the abbreviation '*Ind. Est*'. Industry and warehouse units, which tend not to use bulky raw materials.

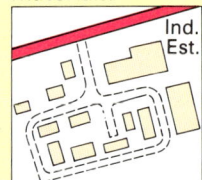

Clues to look for:
1. Location at the edge of towns and cities
2. Location close to main roads and motorways for good transport links

Power stations require large amounts of water for cooling purposes, and are likely to be located near water, often rivers.

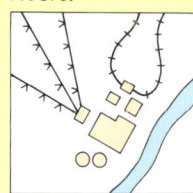

Clues to look for:
1. *Large buildings* and *round cooling towers*
2. Concentration of *power transmission lines* running from them
3. *Rail links* or *jetties* for bringing in raw materials to burn

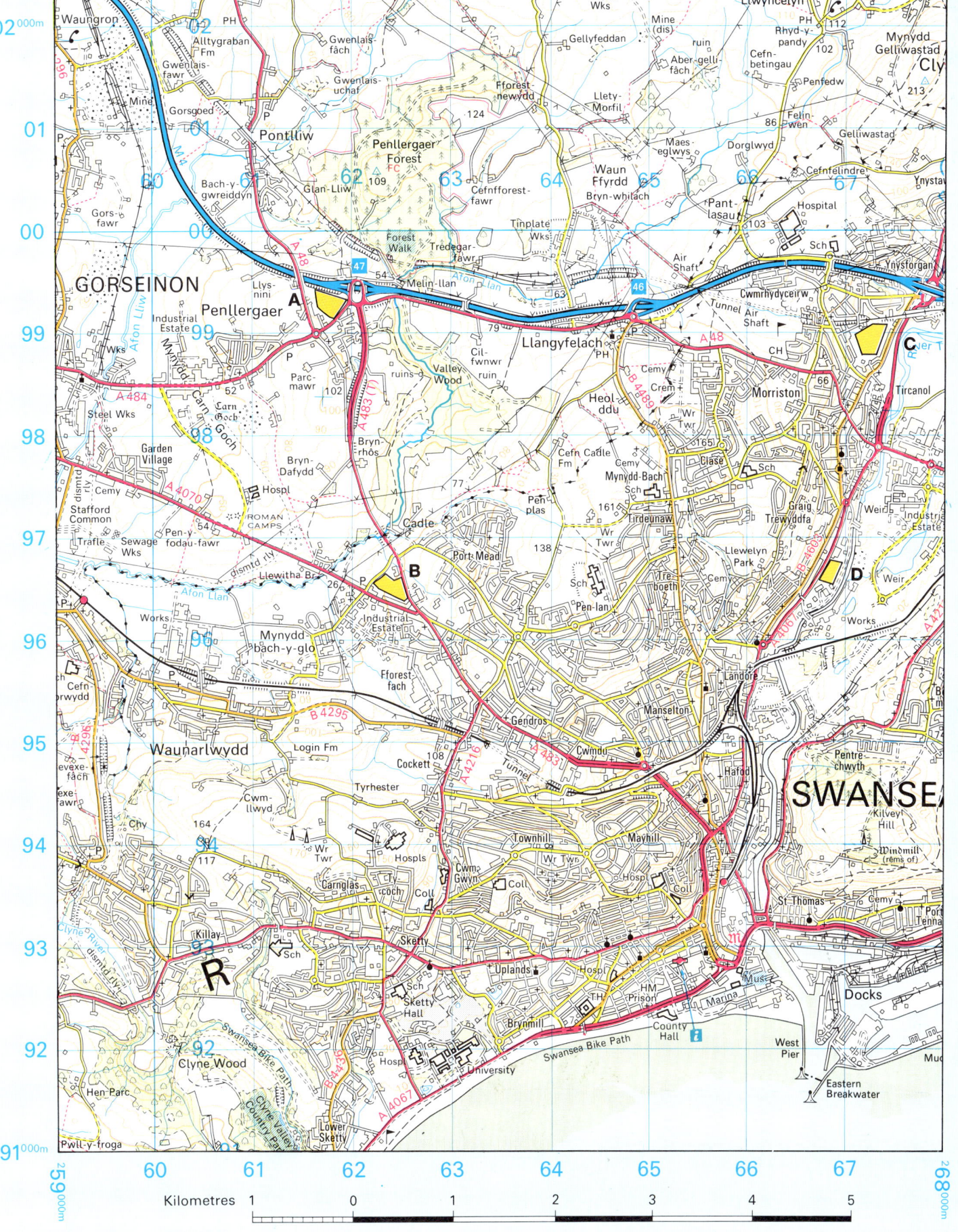

INVESTIGATION 5

Glamorgan
Siting a new supermarket

Briefing

Sainsbury's, Britain's leading food retailer, operates over 270 supermarkets countrywide. Each week 6.5 million people shop at Sainsbury's. Sainsbury's is one of the fastest growing retail companies in Britain. When it comes to developing new supermarkets, Sainsbury's has a clear policy.

Taking Sainsbury's policy into account, your task is to select a site for a new supermarket in the area shown by the map on the previous page.

Work in a small group for Work programmes **A** and **B**, and on your own for the **Report back** programme.

Work programme A
What is Sainsbury's supermarket development policy?

The company's policy is outlined by the people on the opposite page. Read through all their comments carefully.
- Based on those comments, make a list of all the locational factors that need to be taken into account when locating a new supermarket. You might find these headings useful: **size, access, environmental impact**.
- When you have completed your list, discuss how important you think each factor should be. For each factor decide if it is

      * * * Very important
        * * Important
          * Less important

Work programme B
Selecting a site

Land is available at four possible sites. These four sites are shown in yellow on the map on the previous page.
- Take each site in turn, and consider to what extent it meets the locational factors you have already identified. Make notes as you discuss each site.
- As a group select the site which you think is the best.

Report back

When the group has selected a site, each group member should:
- Write a short report, which outlines the advantages, and possible disadvantages of the chosen site. Make sure that you have covered all the locational factors your group identified.
- Draw a map of the area which shows the chosen supermarket site. Add notes to your map which help to explain why it is a good site for a supermarket.

The Sainsbury's supermarket on the Oxford ring road

'Planning the location of a new supermarket is of paramount importance. The right site is one that achieves a balance between many different pressures. Finding such a site is difficult. It has to provide easy, and safe, access, and have space enough for a large 30 000 sq ft store and plenty of carparking – there is no point in spending a lot of money developing a site that is too cramped. At the same time we want to think carefully about how it will affect the local community.'

STORE MANAGER

'We do have to remember that not everyone has a car. Ideally a new supermarket can be sited on a bus route. But the most important element nowadays is that the site has good road access. We draw our customers from a wide local area, and we want as many people as possible to be able to reach the store as easily as possible. Remember too that lorries and vans make daily deliveries, from the local area and from nationwide.'

CUSTOMER SERVICES ASSISTANT

'The design and surroundings of a new supermarket is something that needs careful thought. For one thing we don't want to have an unnecessary impact on the local area and the people who already live and work there. Also keeping the right image for Sainsbury's is very important. Sainsbury's has a 'clean, modern, high quality' image, and the surroundings of a new supermarket need to back up this image.'

ARCHITECT

'More and more people now do their food shopping as a once-a-week trip. The food and drink bought by an average household each week is 70–90 lbs, about eight carrier bags worth. Plenty of carparking space close to the store is vital. People prefer level carparking, not multi-storey which is much less convenient when carrying heavy shopping loads. Convenient, level carparking is probably the most important thing for most superstore customers'

MARKET RESEARCHER

'Using the car for shopping is the preferred method of transport for most people. To find a site with enough room for level carparking means that we tend to look for edge-of-town or out-of-town locations. Land isolated by new road systems is often suitable for supermarket development.'

SURVEYOR

6 MAPSKILLS

ASSIGNMENT 6: Buckinghamshire
Flows and movements

People and goods are constantly on the move.
- Each year millions of people visit other countries on holiday
- Each day thousands of vehicles are on the move on the roads
- During the day there is an ever changing pattern of pedestrian movements along the streets of a town

These are just three examples of flows and movements. Three techniques for mapping flows and movements are outlined below.

Line links

The airline route map below is an example of the line link technique. Each line on the globe represents one of BA's route links from London to another part of the world.

This technique can be used to show:
- Simple links between places – one line for each link. For example, there are flights from London to New York.
- The number of links or movements – one line for each movement.

For example, if the number of flights from London to New York was twelve and the number of flights from London to Mexico City was two, there would be twelve lines for the former and two lines for the latter.

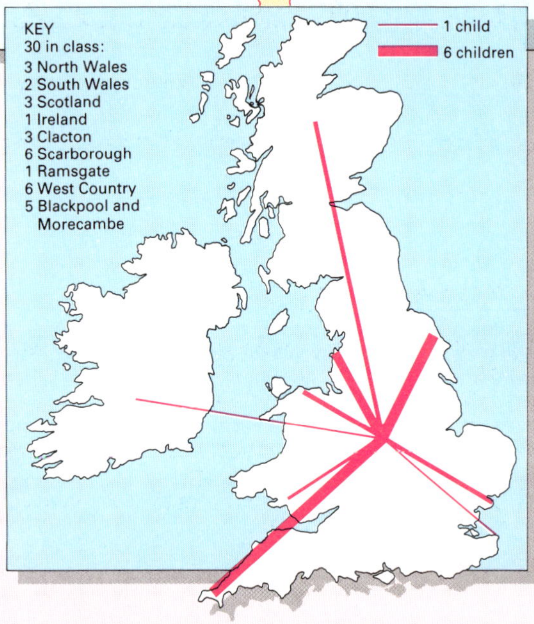

KEY
30 in class:
3 North Wales
2 South Wales
3 Scotland
1 Ireland
3 Clacton
6 Scarborough
1 Ramsgate
6 West Country
5 Blackpool and Morecambe

— 1 child
━ 6 children

Flow diagrams

A technique used to show the number, or volume, of movements along particular routes.

Using a scale, the thickness of the line is drawn in proportion to the number of movements, or the volume of the flow.

The example on the left shows a flow diagram for the destinations of school children going on holiday.

Number contours

This technique, shown on the opposite page, is used to show how the numbers of something vary over a particular area. Drawing number contours is a way of showing a generalised pattern.

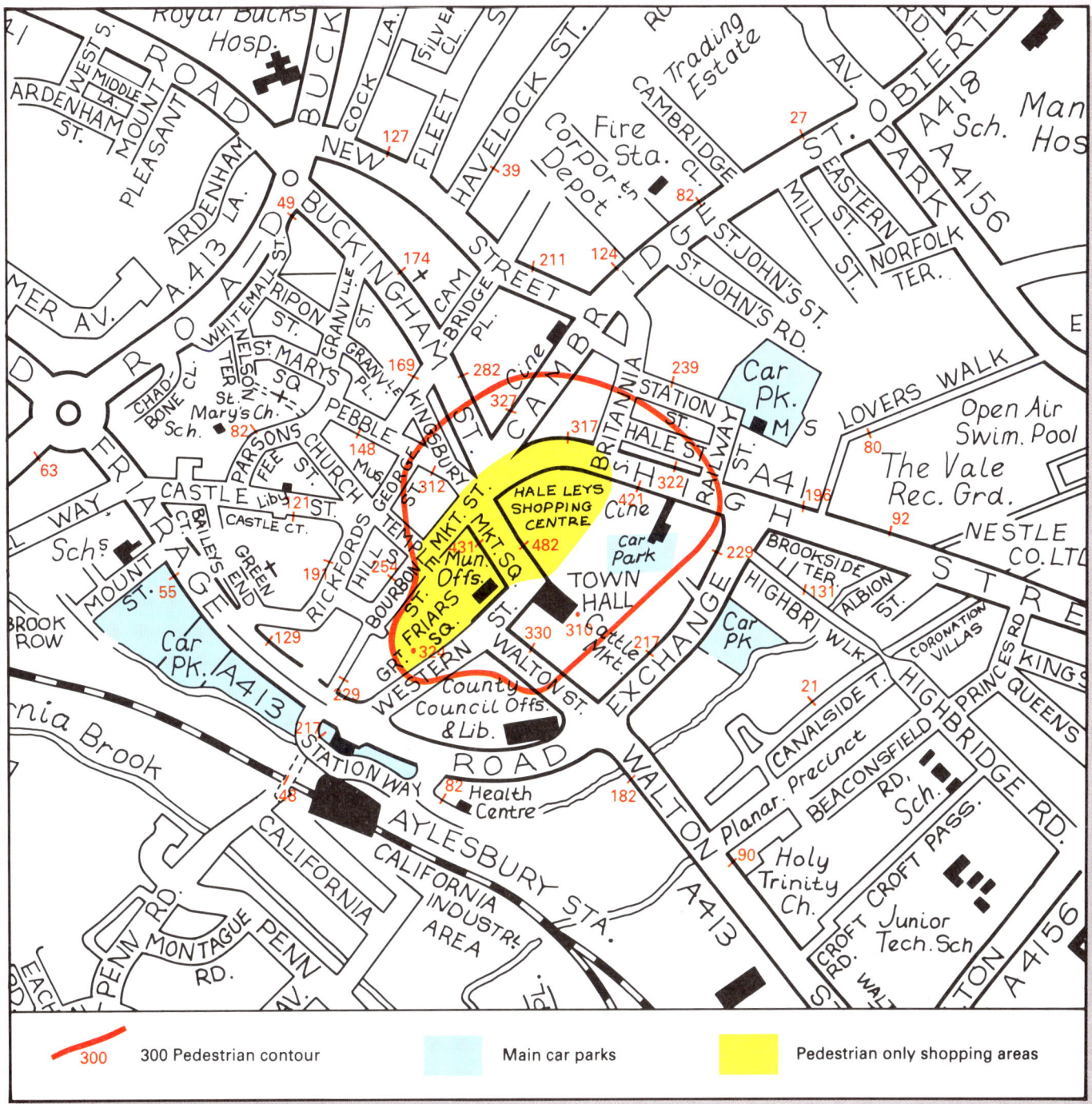

Test your skill

The map above shows the town centre of Aylesbury. The figures give the number of pedestrians passing certain points, during a 15 minute count, on a normal weekday mid-morning.

A number contour line has already been drawn to enclose the part of the town centre where over 300 people passed the count point in that 15 minute period.

1. Place a sheet of tracing paper over the map. Draw a number contour map, by constructing number contours for these values: 400 ... 300 ... 200 ... 100.

2. Describe the pattern that your map shows.

3. What conclusions can you draw from the pattern on your map?
   What factors might help to explain the map pattern?

4. How might you expect the pattern to be different:
   a on a wet Sunday afternoon?
   b at lunchtime on one of the last shopping days before Christmas?

6 INVESTIGATION

Traffic flows in Aylesbury
Buckinghamshire

Briefing

Aylesbury, in Buckinghamshire, is a prosperous and expanding town. In 1977 it had a population of about 50 000. By 1991 it is predicted that it will have a population of about 60 000. Employment opportunities in the town have increased to match the growing population.

But, like other similarly placed towns, growth has brought with it increased traffic problems. Your task in this investigation is to look at how traffic flows in Aylesbury will increase, and to predict future traffic trouble spots.

Report back

At the end of the investigation you should have completed your own flow map and a written report.

Work programme A
1977 measured traffic flows

Working on your own, look at the outline map on the opposite page which shows the pattern of main roads in Aylesbury. The figures in the circles on the map show the number of vehicles (in thousands) using the roads per day – as they were measured in 1977.

- On your own copy of the road map, construct a flow map to show the 1977 vehicle information.
  Use a scale of 1mm to 1000 vehicles.

Work programme B
Predicting future traffic trouble spots

In 1977 traffic movement, although slow during morning and evening rush hours, was generally satisfactory. The road system was just about coping. However, it was clear to the planners that the volume of vehicles was going to increase. It was thought that, in particular, traffic would increase on main roads leading in and out of Aylesbury.

Working on your own:

- Look at your 1977 flow map.
  Where are the possible future traffic congestion trouble spots?
  Which road junctions in the Aylesbury road system are going to have to cope with the greatest number of vehicles?
- Make a prediction of the three or four points in the road system where future traffic congestion will be most serious.
  Mark your predicted points on your flow map.
- You have not had all that much information to go on when making your prediction. Make a list of the further information you would want to have in order to make a more detailed prediction of future traffic congestion points.

Rush hour in Aylesbury

Work programme C
1991 predicted traffic flows

The figures at the foot of the opposite page are what the planners predict the traffic flows will be in 1991.

Again, working on your own:

- Use this data to widen the flow lines on your existing 1977 flow map. Use the same scale, but a different colour to show the difference between the 1977 and 1991 data
- Compare, in writing, the 1977 measured flows and the 1991 predicted flows. For example:
  where is it predicted that traffic will increase most?
  where is it predicted that traffic will increase least rapidly?
- In the light of the planners' predicted figures, do you need to revise your own predictions on future traffic trouble spots?
  Give the full reasons for your answer.

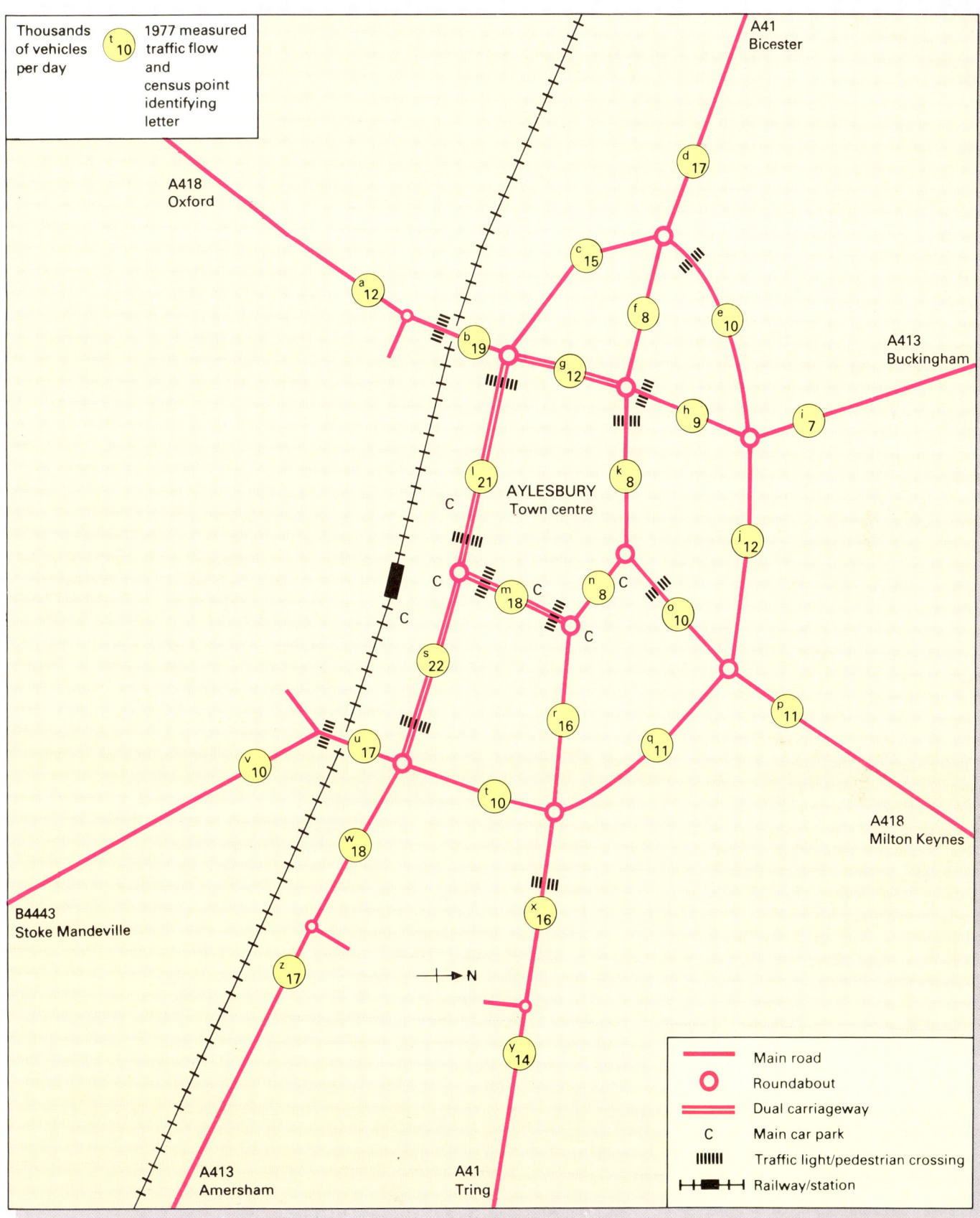

1991: Predicted traffic flows

a: 19 b: 28 c: 19 d: 27 e: 10 f: 5 g: 22 h: 8 i: 9 j: 11 k: 15 l: 38 m: 26 n: 12 o: 14 p: 18 q: 13
r: 18 s: 33 t: 13 u: 24 v: 16 w: 24 x: 27 y: 24 z: 20

7 MAPSKILLS

Assignment 7: Gloucestershire
Interpreting the rural landscape

In most of Britain's lowland countryside, intensive crop and animal farming is the main use of the land. In upland areas the land is more likely to be used for sheep farming, forestry, or the land is left as moorland.

Farming

OS maps, like the ones in this book, give us some, but not very much, information about farming land-use. One problem for map-makers is that farmers change the use of their fields, and so any map of agricultural land-use can quickly go out-of-date.

The OS 1:50 000 maps tell us little about farming, but give us a few clues:
- the number of farms can indicate the importance of farming in that area
- the spacing of farms can indicate the size of farms

Unfortunately, not all farms are marked on 1:50 000 maps.

The larger scale 1:25 000 maps provide more detailed information.
- All the farms are named, and field boundaries are shown
- A few types of land-use are marked – woodland types particularly

Forestry

Woods and copses are found in most parts of Britain. Large scale commercial forestry, however, is an important economic activity only in some upland areas, where large stands of coniferous trees have been planted.

Look for the word *plantation*, straight edges to the forested area, and criss-crossing vehicle tracks – all are evidence of commercial forestry.

Recreation

In parts of the countryside more land is now being used for recreation and tourism purposes – only some of these activities are shown on OS maps. Look out for the blue tourist information symbols on OS 1:50 000 maps; look too for hotels, golf courses, and National Trust land.

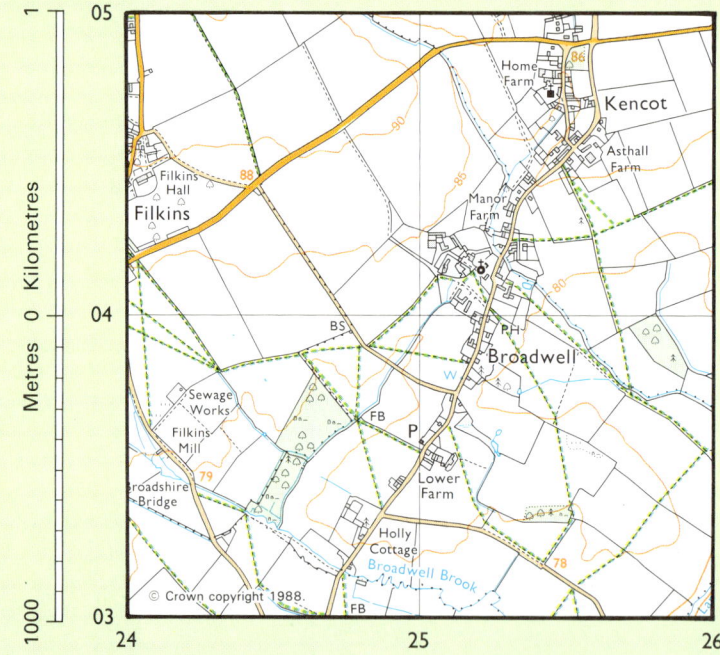

Test your skills 1
Farming

The 1:25 000 map on this page is a larger scale map of 4 grid squares on the 1:50 000 map opposite – locate these four grid squares on that map.

1. **a** How many farms are named in these 4 squares on the 1:50 000 map?
   b How many farms are named on the 1:25 000 map?

2. **a** Compare the size of the fields in grid square 2503 with those in grid square 2404.
   b Suggest a possible reason, or reasons, for the differences.

3. Say how the land is being used at these locations – check with the 1:25 000 symbols key on page 47 if you need to.
   a 258039 **b** 241043 **c** 247036
   d 255036 **e** 254047 **f** 242037

4. Mixed crop and animal farming is carried out in this area. What map evidence is there that cereal crops have traditionally been grown here?

Test your skill 2
Recreational land-use

Using the 1:50 000 map on the opposite page:

1. The map gives information about two facilities in Upper Inglesham (2096) which might be useful to holiday-makers. What are they?

2. Give the map square references of six other pieces of tourist information on the map.

3. There are a number of lakes shown on the map. What evidence is there that they are man-made?

Test your skill 3
Rural services

1. Find the village of Langford (2402). According to the map, what services or facilities are available in the village?

2. Langford has a population of 280 people. What other services or facilities might you reasonably expect to find in a village of this size (but which the map does not show)?

3. The local bus now goes through Langford twice a week. What other form of public transport had been available to villagers in the past?

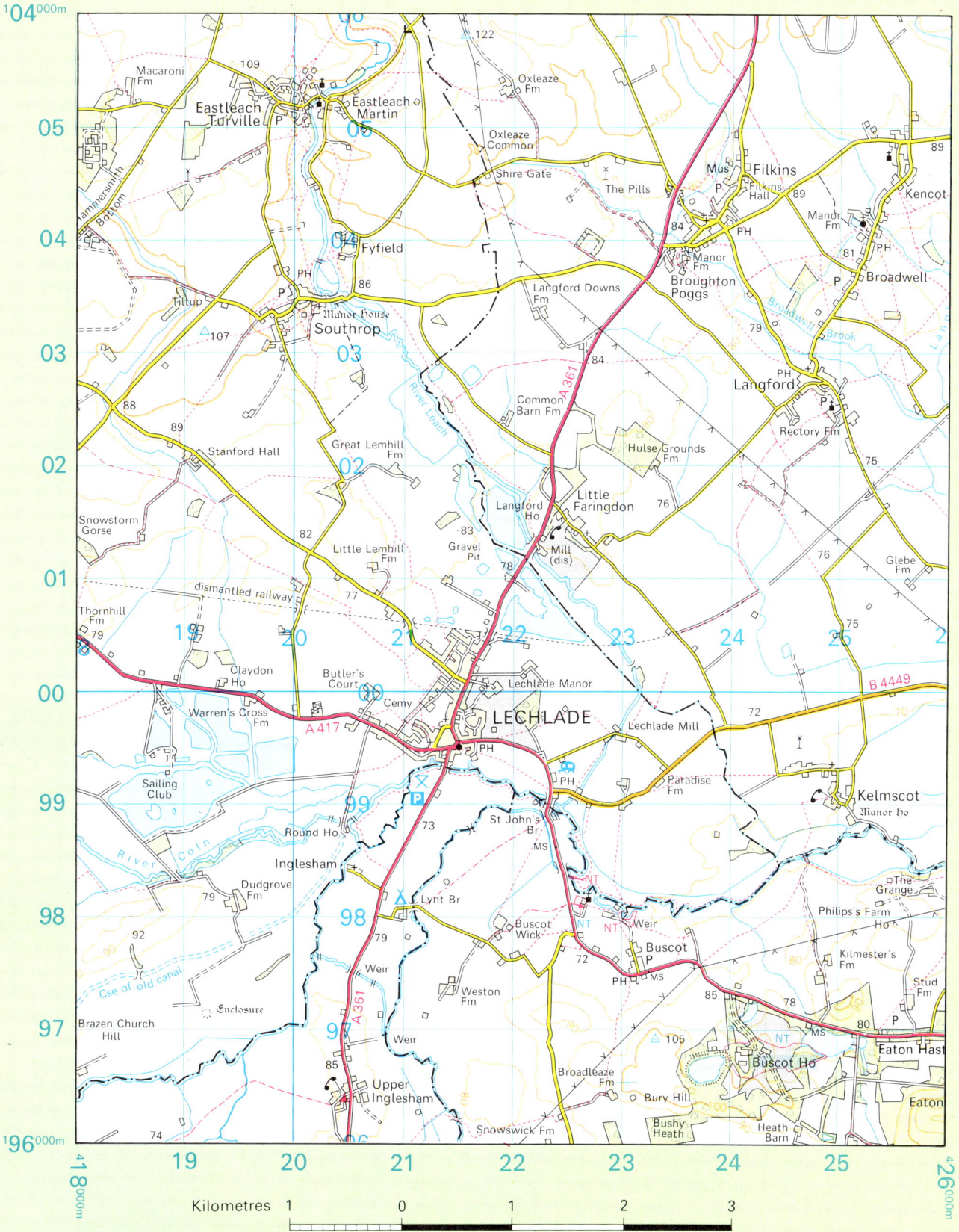

7 INVESTIGATION

A Leisure Park for Lechlade?
Gloucestershire

Briefing

The picturesque small town of Lechlade is situated on the River Thames. On two sides of the town there are large gravel pit workings. The gravel pits are not pretty, but until now they have not had that much effect on Lechlade. Now all that could change.

Amy Roadstone Corporation (ARC) have drawn up plans to develop their gravel pit site into a 200 acre Leisure Park, right on the edge of the town. Most local people are up in arms about what they call a 'horrific' plan. Your task is to consider the issues involved in this Leisure Park proposal.

Work programmes A-E

Work in a pair or small group to complete all the work programmes.
In your group decide on the most effective way of working.

Report back

You should present a group report at the end of the investigation.
It is up to you to plan the most effective presentation of your report, but it should include maps/diagrams and written (or recorded) information.

A: Where would the Leisure Park be?

The ARC Master Plan is shown on the opposite page. The planned site is north of Lechlade.

Work out the Park's exact location and size on the OS 1:50 000 map on the previous page. Draw your own map to show the location of:
- the Park
- Lechlade, and other settlements that would be affected
- the roads that would carry increased traffic
- any other information that you think is relevant

B: The potential catchment area

ARC's research suggests that the Leisure Park would attract visitors from up to 90 minutes travel time away.

Using the data in the box below, draw a map to show the possible catchment area of the Lechlade Leisure Park.

Within 90 minutes travel time:
West London, Milton Keynes, Northampton, Coventry, South Birmingham, Hereford, Cardiff, Weston-super-Mare, Southampton, Guildford

Within 60 minutes travel time:
High Wycombe, Stratford-upon-Avon, Gloucester, Bristol, Bath, Reading

C: ARC's case

Consider the information in ARC's Master Plan.

What exactly is planned for the 200 acre site?

Put yourself in the place of ARC's Project Manager for the Leisure Park. What arguments would you use to try and persuade
- the district council planners
- the local residents
that the Leisure Park would be a good development for the area?

D: The objectors' case

Using your own ideas, and the objector's letter on this page, outline the arguments that local people could use against allowing the development of the Leisure Park on this site.

E: Making a decision

Many large-scale new developments involve a conflict of interest between different groups of people. The Lechlade Leisure Park proposal is no exception. Weigh up the different sides of the argument.

- If it was up to you, would you allow this particular proposal? Give the full reasons for your decision.
- If you would not allow this proposal, would you allow any development on this site? Outline your ideas as fully as you can.

The Director of Planning
Cotswold District Council
Cirencester
Gloucestshire

Dear Sir,

PROPOSED LECHLADE 'LEISURE PARK'

I am writing to you as a local resident to object to this plan. The scheme visualises building 300 chalets, 250 caravan sites, and "amusement park" (permanent fairground?), pub, fast-food outlet, garage, shops, "garden centre", parking for over 2000 cars etc etc. This is a monstrous scheme, quite out of keeping with the size of Lechlade and the dignity of the surrounding countryside. Lechlade is traditionally the nearest settlement to the source of the Thames, and is a noted attraction to visitors from all over the world. The Cotswold area, in which Lechlade lies, is to many visitors the perfect image of rural England.

There will be a lot of local hostility to the proposal, I dare say from everyone, except perhaps local tradespeople. Allowing this proposal would:

* Make the local traffic problems worse.
* Put extreme pressure on local parking, which will affect local people who use Lechlade for shopping etc.
* Probably bring down-market places of entertainment to the town, such as amusement arcades, takeaways, discotheques, which would result in late-night activity and music.
* The large, and unwelcome, number of trippers attracted by the Park would include a high proportion of undesirables.
* Mean worsening security in terms of break-ins, poaching and trespass.
* Bring a worsening of an already bad refuse and litter problem.
* Be a pollution threat to the local rivers and lakes.
* Involve a down-grading and devaluing of all property in the area.

The proposed Leisure Park must not be allowed to happen. From being its present dignified and homely place, typifying the Best of Britain, Lechlade would be turned into a sort of "Clacton-on-Thames" with all the problems of congestion, litter and noise.

Yours faithfully,

The centre of Lechlade

FACT SHEET

300 holiday chalets
250 caravan sites
16 houseboats
130 houses for permanent occupation

Amusement park of 8.7 acres. Pub, fast-food outlet, restaurant, garage, garden centre, shops. Car parking for 2000 cars.

1. Holiday villages (×3)
2. Restaurant, pub and village shops
3. Car parks (×3)
4. Sailing club
5. Trout farm
6. Petrol station and burger bar
7. Information Centre
8. Garden centre
9. Picnic area
10. Amusement area
11. Children's play area
12. Tennis courts
13. Caravan park
14. Houseboat moorings
15. Residential housing

MAPSKILLS 8

ASSIGNMENT 8: Cumbria
Contours and relief

The landscape in any area is a combination of the work of people and the effects of nature. Settlements, farming and industry are all part of the *human landscape*. The shape of the land is part of the natural, or *physical landscape*.

The shape of the physical landscape in an area is called its **relief**. Using **contour lines**, and other information about height, we can use an OS map to 'see' what the relief and landscape of an area is like without actually being there.

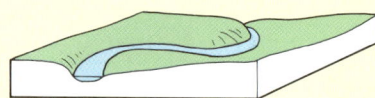
Flat relief

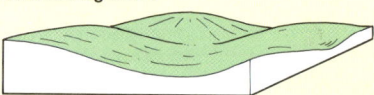
Undulating relief

Hilly relief

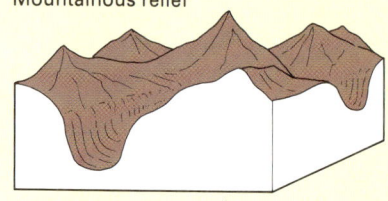
Mountainous relief

The height of the land

In order to draw an OS map the height of the land has to be carefully surveyed.

Certain points are accurately measured. **Spot heights** (like the one in Square 2999 in Extract A on the other page) and **triangulation points** (as in Extract A Square 2797) show the accurately measured height of that place above sea level.

Contour lines show the height of the rest of the landscape. The 200m contour line runs along a line of land that is exactly 200m above sea level. So the land on one side must be lower than 200m, while the land on the other side must be higher than 200m.

All over the map some contour lines will have their heights marked – in metres above sea level. You can work out the height of any other contour from those that do have their height marked.

- The height gap (the *contour interval*) between contour lines is 10m on OS 1:50 000 maps (5m on OS 1:25 000 maps).
- At regular 50m intervals the contours are printed in a heavier line.

The spacing of the contours tell us something about the steepness of the slope.

- The closer together the contours, the steeper the slope
- The further apart the contours, the gentler the slope

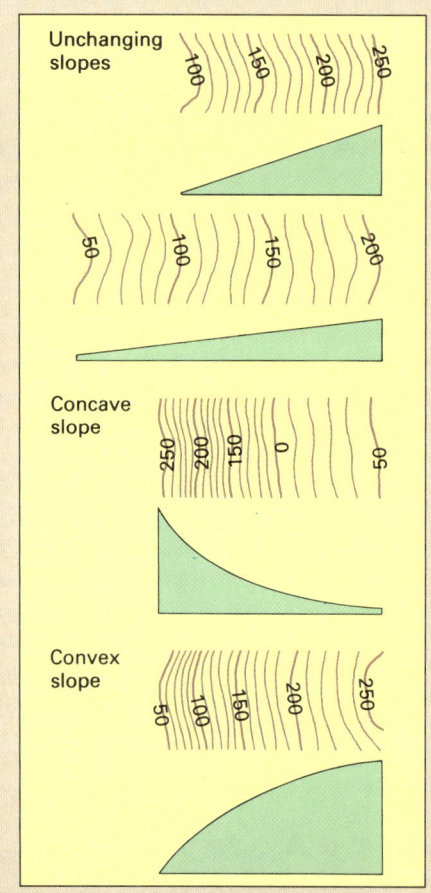

Simple contour patterns do not occur all that often in practice. Landscapes have their own individual and complex shapes! Yet in using contours to interpret the relief of an area, there are some simple steps you can follow.

1 Look for the highest points – usually they will be hill tops
2 Look for the lowest points – often in valleys where there are rivers and lakes
3 Look for where the steepest slopes are found – where the contours are most closely spaced
4 Work out which way the land is sloping – use the contour heights

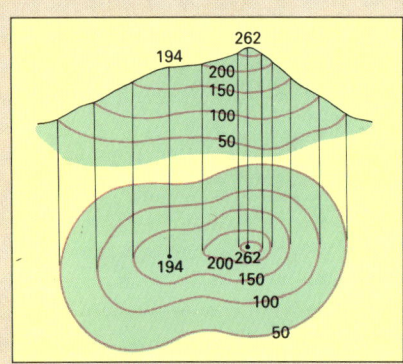

Test your skill 1

On the opposite page there are two small extracts from OS 1:50 000 maps. From the number of contour lines shown it is clear that both maps show areas of high relief.

Carry out this exercise for both map extracts in turn.

1 What is the highest point in the area? What is its height?
2 Where is the lowest point? What is its approximate height?
3 In which grid squares are the steepest slopes? In which direction is the land sloping?
4 Using **Extract A**, would you be walking uphill or downhill if you:
 a walked east from 275978?
 b walked south from 263990?
 c walked north east from 271986?
5 Using **Extract B**, draw a simple sketch map of the area, which shows
 - high points and low points
 - the direction of slopes in the area (use arrows to show this information – remember: land usually slopes down towards rivers)

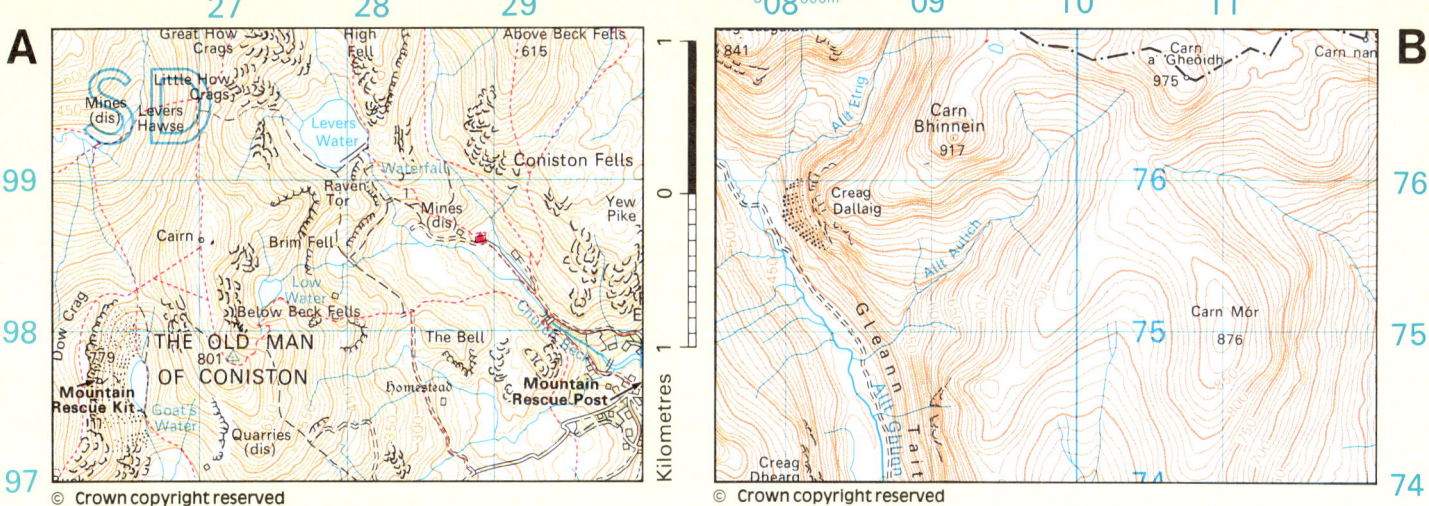

Slope Patterns

When using contours to interpret slopes, look out for:
- the **pattern** of contours – are they straight or rounded?
- the **spacing** between contours – how steep is the slope?
- the **height** of the contours – which direction is the land sloping?

The direction of river flow

It will not come as a great surprise to you that rivers always flow downhill! In fact it is a useful thought to keep in mind when interpreting contours and relief.

On the right are some clues to look out for when working out the direction a river or stream is flowing.

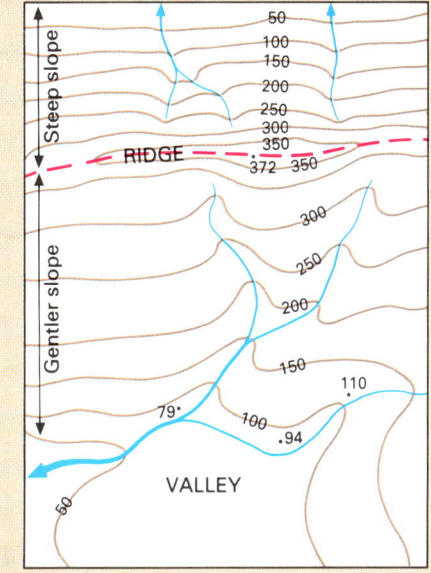

The **high ground** which divides the streams of two river systems is called the **watershed**.

Where **contour lines cross a river** they point **upstream**.

Tributaries joining a river usually point **downstream**.

Spot heights near river show ground becoming lower in a downstream direction.

Rivers become wider downstream, especially near their **mouth**.

Test your skill 2

Using Map extract B above:
1. Describe the direction and shape of the slopes between these points:
   a 089761 and 085752
   b 110755 and 115764
2. a Is the stream in square 1175 flowing north west or south east?
   b What about the stream in square 0975?

Calculating gradient

The road that runs over Hardknott Pass in Cumbria is one of the steepest sections of public road in Britain – any steeper and it would be impassable to ordinary cars. The road has a *gradient* of 1:3.

A gradient of 1:3 means that for every 3m along the ground, the land rises or falls 1m.

This is how to calculate the gradient of a slope on an OS map.

To work out the gradient between points A and B

1. Use the map scale to measure the ground distance between A and B – in **metres**. Remember: on 1:50 000 maps the scale is 2cm:1km or 1000m

   This example: Distance AB = 1500m

2. Work out the difference in land height between A and B, using contours or spot heights.

   This example: A is at 475m, B is at 150m
   Height Difference = 325m

3. Gradients are given as '1-in-something', so divide the ground distance by the height difference.

   This example: 1500 ÷ 375 = 4
   Gradient between A and B is 1:4

Test your skill 3

Work out the gradient between these points:
- Between points X and Y on the diagram on the left
- Extract B: between the top of the Old Man of Coniston (272978) and a point due east at 282978
- Extract A: the top of Carn Mor (1175) and 119742

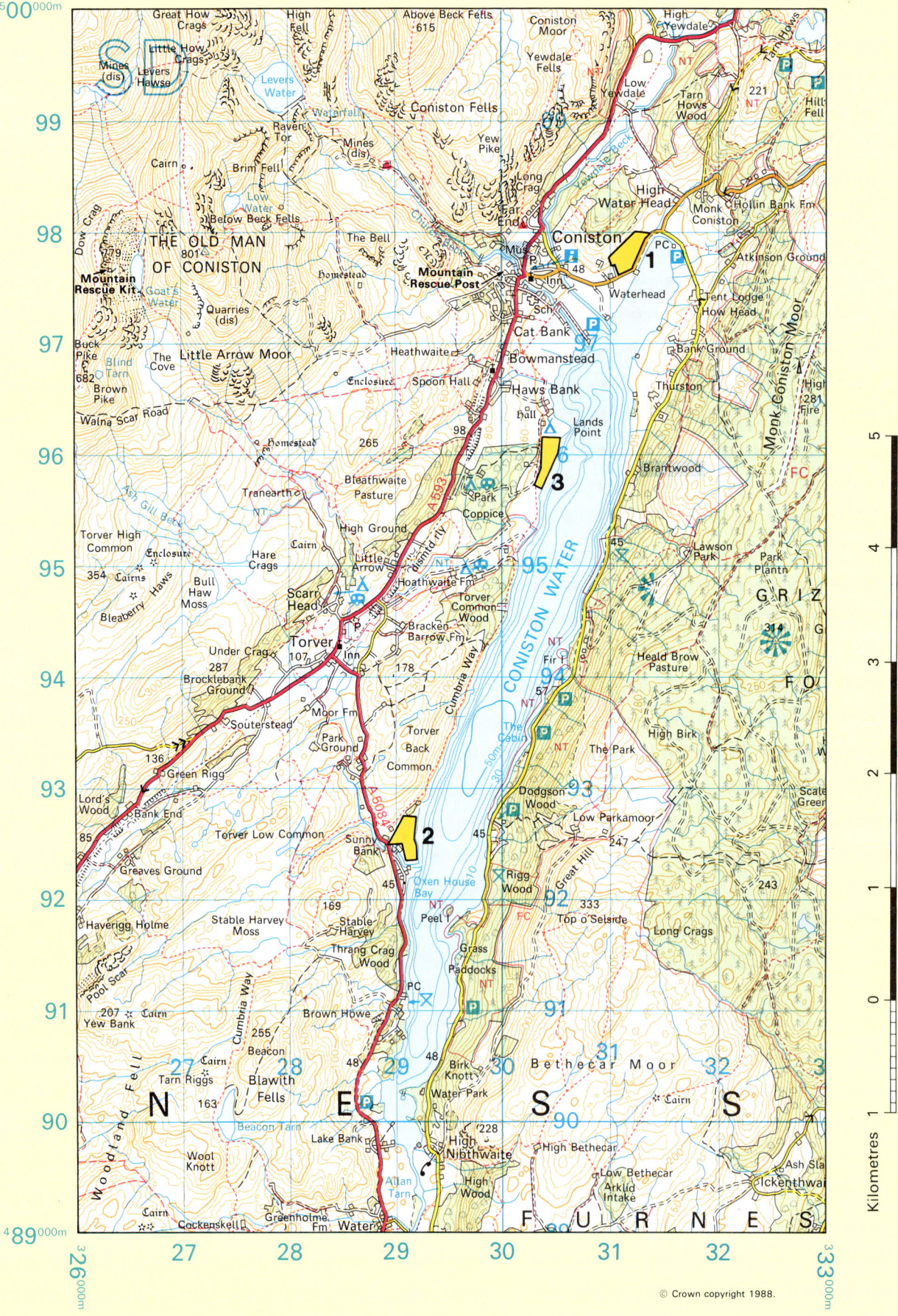

Cumbria
Siting a new leisure holiday complex

INVESTIGATION 8

Briefing

Coniston Water is one of the lakes in the English Lake District of Cumbria. The Lake District, with its spectacular lake and mountain scenery, is one of the most popular tourist areas in Britain. Coniston Water, where in the 1960s Donald Campbell was killed while trying to beat the world water speed record, is one of the lakes on which boating and water sports are allowed.

Northern Construction plc wants to develop a new holiday homes complex in the Coniston area. There is some information below about NC's plans for its Lakelands Leisure Complex.

You have been engaged by NC as a consultant. Your job is to advise the company about the best site for the Lakelands Leisure Complex.

Report back

Present your work as a report to **Northern Construction**. Your report will include a map and written information.

Coniston Water

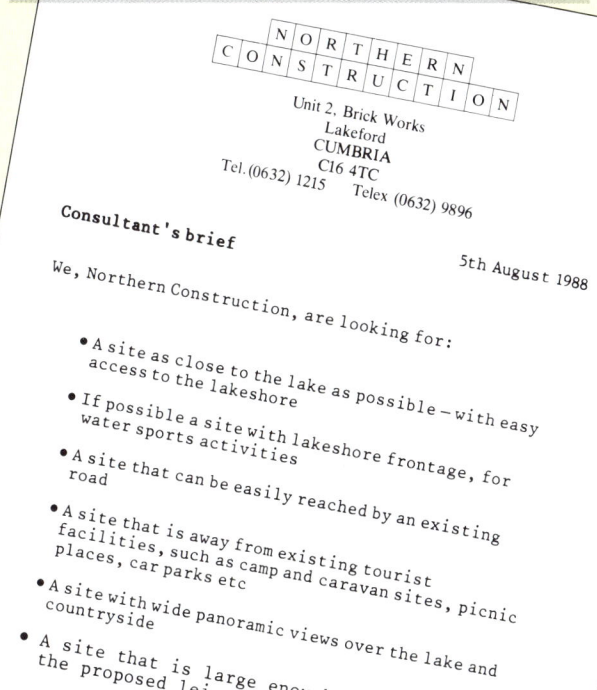

NORTHERN CONSTRUCTION
Unit 2, Brick Works
Lakeford
CUMBRIA
C16 4TC
Tel. (0632) 1215   Telex (0632) 9896

Consultant's brief   5th August 1988

We, Northern Construction, are looking for:

- A site as close to the lake as possible – with easy access to the lakeshore
- If possible a site with lakeshore frontage, for water sports activities
- A site that can be easily reached by an existing road
- A site that is away from existing tourist facilities, such as camp and caravan sites, picnic places, car parks etc
- A site with wide panoramic views over the lake and countryside
- A site that is large enough to accommodate the proposed leisure complex facilities.

Work programmes A, B and C
Giving planning advice

Work in a pair or small group.

NC has identified 3 possible sites for its Lakeland Leisure Complex. They are shown on the OS map:
- Site 1 – square 3197
- Site 2 – square 2992
- Site 3 – squares 3095 / 3096

In order to select the best site NC has listed the things it is looking for in a *Consultant's Brief*.

A: Mapping
Read the Consultant's Brief carefully.
For your report draw a map of the Coniston area which includes any information you think NC would want to know. Your map must show the lake and the 3 sites, plus the other things mentioned in the Brief.

B: Evaluating
Use the Brief to consider the suitability of each site. One way to do this is to give each site a score out of 5 for each of the things listed in the Brief. However, it is up to you to decide on the most effective way of choosing the best site.

In your report you must write about the advantages and disadvantages of each site, and recommend to NC the one you think would be best.

C: Research
NC are also interested in what local people would think about the planned Lakeland Leisure Complex. In your report suggest an effective way that NC could set about finding out local peoples' views.

LAKELANDS LEISURE COMPLEX
– beside lovely Coniston Water...

- 100 Luxurious holiday apartments
- The centre's own superb restaurant
- Tennis courts and squash court
- Health and fitness centre with sauna
- Heated indoor swimming pool
- Set in beautiful unspoilt countryside
- Sailing sail-boarding and water skiing

MAPSKILLS 9

ASSIGNMENT 9: Tayside
Drawing cross-sections

A *cross-section*, or cut-away view, across an area can be drawn using contour heights.

With a bit of practice you can sketch cross-sections by eye, by just looking at the pattern of contours.
The way to draw an accurate cross-section is explained below.

An accurately drawn cross-section can tell us if two points are *intervisible*.

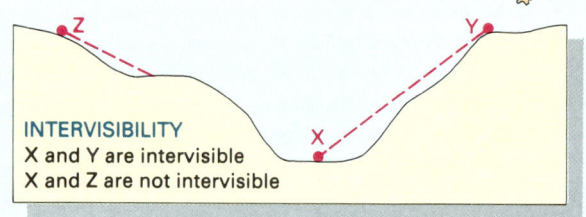

INTERVISIBILITY
X and Y are intervisible
X and Z are not intervisible

How to draw a cross-section from A to B

1. Before you start look carefully at the area of the cross-section.
   - Where are the *highest* and *lowest* points?
   - In which *directions* is the land sloping?
   - Remember: a river is at the *lowest point in a valley*

2. Place a sheet of paper along the line of the cross-section. On the paper mark where the contours cut the line of the cross-section. Mark on the contour heights – either by looking at the map, or by working them out. Mark on the position of important features such as rivers.
   - If the contours are closely spaced, you don't have to mark on every contour – use the heavy contours at 50m intervals.

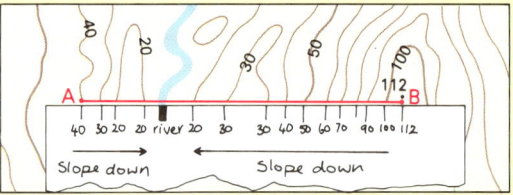

3. Draw a base, exactly the same width as the cross-section. Decide on a height (or vertical) scale to mark up the side.
   - Be careful not to *over exaggerate* the height scale – about 2–4cm between the highest and lowest points is enough
   - Remember to write in the *height scale* you are using

4. Using the marks on the edge of your piece of paper, mark the heights in on your base – each cross must be directly above the mark on your paper.

5. Finally, join up the height crosses in a smooth curve. Name any important features, such as rivers or hills.

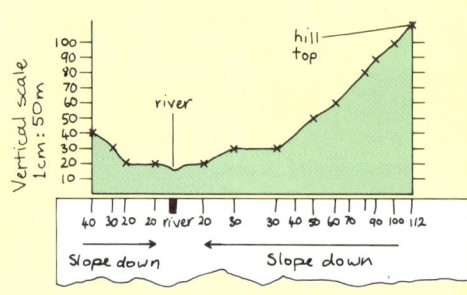

Test your skill 1
Drawing cross-sections

Using the OS 1:50 000 map on the opposite page.

1. **a** Draw an accurate cross-section between the summits of Ben Gulabin (101722) and Ben Earb (079692).
   - As the contours are very closely spaced, for your cross-section only use the heavy contours at 50m intervals
   - Note the position of the river on your finished cross-section

   b Describe the shape of the slopes and river valley (although it is not named on the map, the river is called the Shee Water).

2. **a** Now try drawing a slightly more complicated cross-section – from Carn Aosda (134792) to Carn Bhinnein (092763).
   Be careful – you will come across some contours more than once.
   b Mark the location of Loch Vrotachan and any streams on your cross-section.
   c In clear weather are Carn Aosda and Carn Bhinnein intervisible?

3. Now try some sketch cross-sections – drawing them by eye rather than by accurate measurement.
   a Along the grid line from 100750 to 120750.
   b From the summit of the Cairnwell (1377) to the peak at Carn nan Sac (1176).

Test your skill 2
The physical and human landscape

Using the OS 1:50 000 map on the opposite page.

1. What physical features would you find on the mountainsides at:
   a 121776? **b** 103715? **c** 120735? **d** 087770?

2. In which direction is the main river (the one in the south western corner of the map) flowing? What evidence from the map supports your answer?

3. What evidence is there from the map that tourism is important to the local economy in both summer and winter?

4. Write a detailed description of the relief of the area shown on the map – check back with the notes on previous page if you need to.

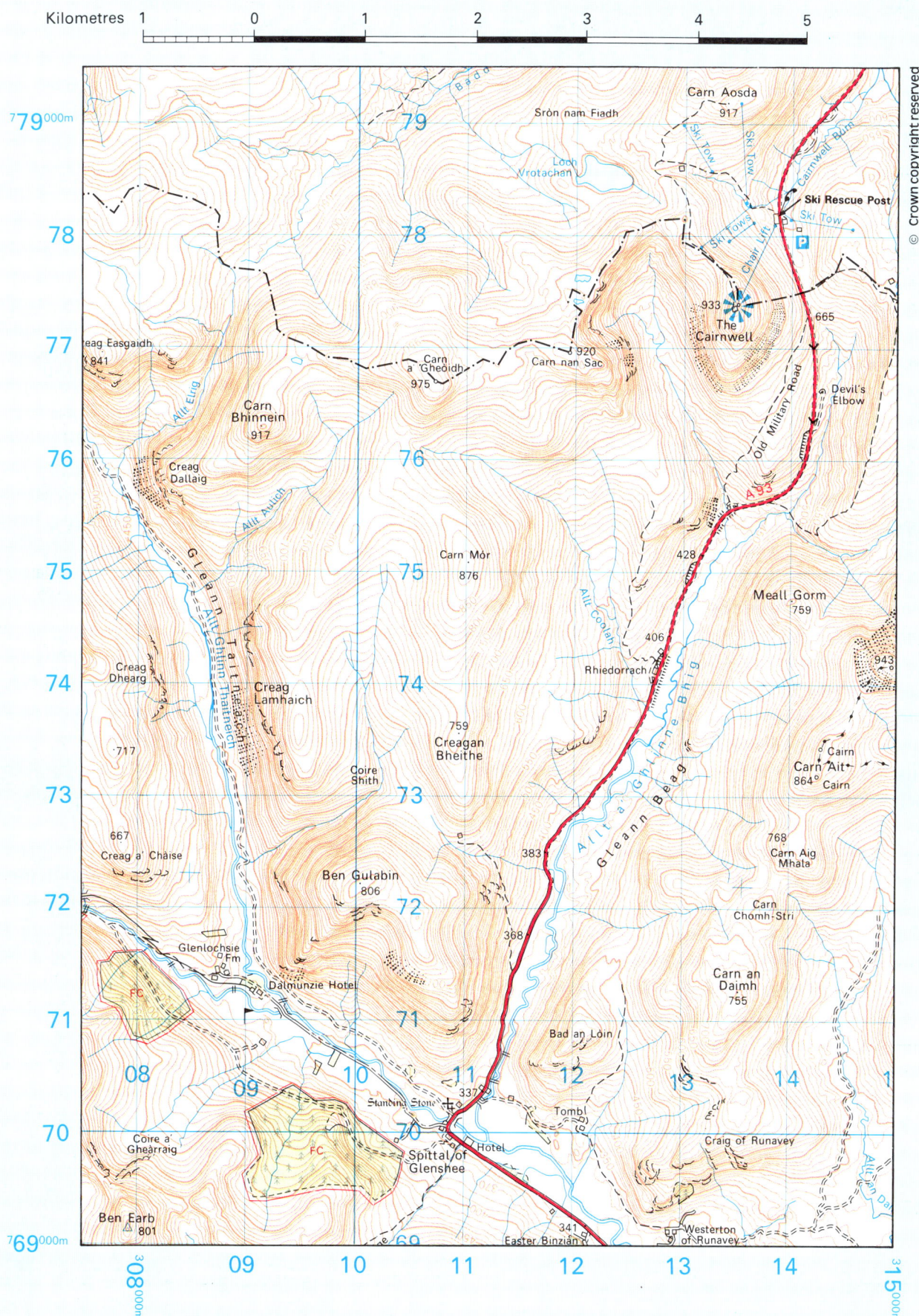

INVESTIGATION 9

Planning a new ski centre in Glenshee Tayside

Briefing

Skiing has become big business in the Scottish Highlands. The largest ski centre is at Aviemore, where there are extensive residential holiday facilities for winter (and summer) activities.

Compared to Aviemore, the development of ski facilities in Glenshee (which are shown on the 1:50 000 map on the previous page) is on a much smaller scale. There are a number of ski lifts, but no on-site residential facilities at Glenshee, and so people drive to the centre to spend the day skiing.

The demand for skiing holidays in Scotland continues to increase. A consortium of building and leisure industry companies, **Scotski**, is interested in developing another ski centre in the Glenshee area. As a consultant to Scotski, your task is advise them by investigating the potential of the area, and assessing the changes any developments might bring to that area.

Work programmes A and B

Work in a pair or in a small group, to do **all** the work programmes

Background work

Before you can begin your investigation and planning work, **everyone** in your group must:
- Be absolutely clear about what Scotski wants to develop. Their ideas are outlined in their **brief** – read it carefully.
- Understand how a ski centre operates. The **maps** below show the existing Glenshee/Cairnwell centre – study the maps and notes carefully.

Report back

At the end of your investigation you need to produce a report for Scotski. The report will contain your ideas, backed up by the necessary maps, diagrams and visuals.

A: Investigating and planning

The base map on the opposite page shows the area Scotski is interested in. This base map is a double-size version of part of the OS 1:50 000 map on the previous page.

- Make one, or more, copies of this base map for your planning work. As you plan you will need to add further information from the OS map onto your base maps.

Using the OS map consider the ski potential of the identified area.

On your base map plan:
- the possible development of ski lifts and ski runs
- the development of the necessary back-up facilities (roads etc)

You must keep Scotski's brief in mind as you plan.

B: Assessing the impact on the local area

How do you think that your planned ski centre would affect:
- the local environment (remember: it is not always winter)
- the local people and community

How do you think that different people in the local community might react to your development plans?

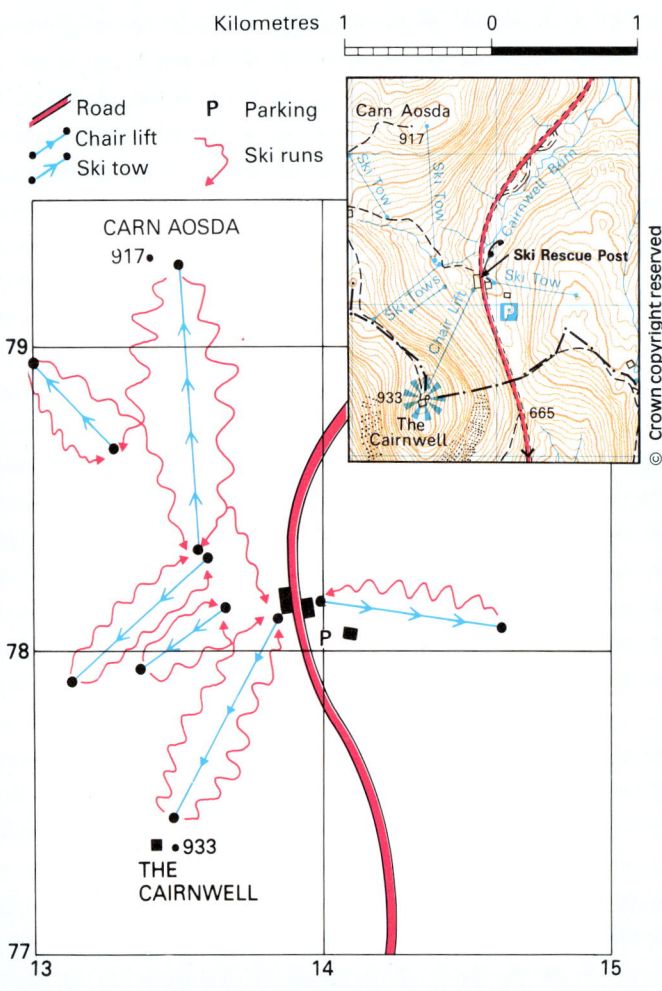

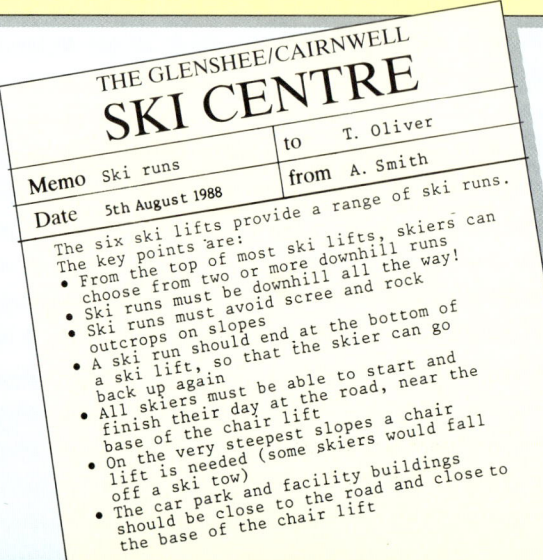

THE GLENSHEE/CAIRNWELL
SKI CENTRE

Memo Ski runs   to T. Oliver
Date 5th August 1988   from A. Smith

The six ski lifts provide a range of ski runs. The key points are:
- From the top of most ski lifts, skiers can choose from two or more downhill runs
- Ski runs must be downhill all the way!
- Ski runs must avoid scree and rock outcrops on slopes
- A ski run should end at the bottom of a ski lift, so that the skier can go back up again
- All skiers must be able to start and finish their day at the road, near the base of the chair lift
- On the very steepest slopes a chair lift is needed (some skiers would fall off a ski tow)
- The car park and facility buildings should be close to the road and close to the base of the chair lift

A ski lift at Glenshee

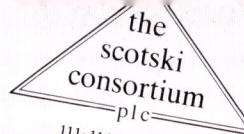

the scotski consortium p l c

111-114 High Street
Dundee
TAYSIDE
Scotland
Tel: (0382) 7153

BRIEF TO CONSULTANT

This is to confirm that you have agreed to act as consultant, and that you will produce a report on the potential for developing a ski centre in the Glenshee/Carn Bhinnein area. It would be useful, at this stage, to go over again what our requirements are.

SIZE

It will be a day ski centre, with the same sort of facilities as at the existing Glenshee/Cairnwell centre.

ROAD ACCESS

A vital element for a day ski centre is that people can reach the centre by road. We are prepared to upgrade existing roads or tracks. We would prefer not to have the expense of constructing long sections of new road, especially on steep slopes.

SKI LIFTS

We are looking to develop 6–8 ski lifts. Our aim is to site the lifts so that there are as many different ski runs as possible. The lifts could include:
- Chair lift – only one chair lift, with a length up to a maximum of 1½ km – chair lift should be used on the steepest slope
- Ski tows – between 5–7 ski tows, with lengths of ½–¾ km – ski tows to be used on medium steep slopes

SKI SLOPE HEIGHTS

Snow cover lasts longer and is most reliable on higher ground,
- the chair lift and at least some ski tows should take skiers up above 850m
- all ski tows should take skiers up to at least 750m, and preferably up to 800m

BACK-UP FACILITIES

There needs to be flat ground near the base of the chair lift for car-parking, and for food/restaurant/ski equipment facilities.

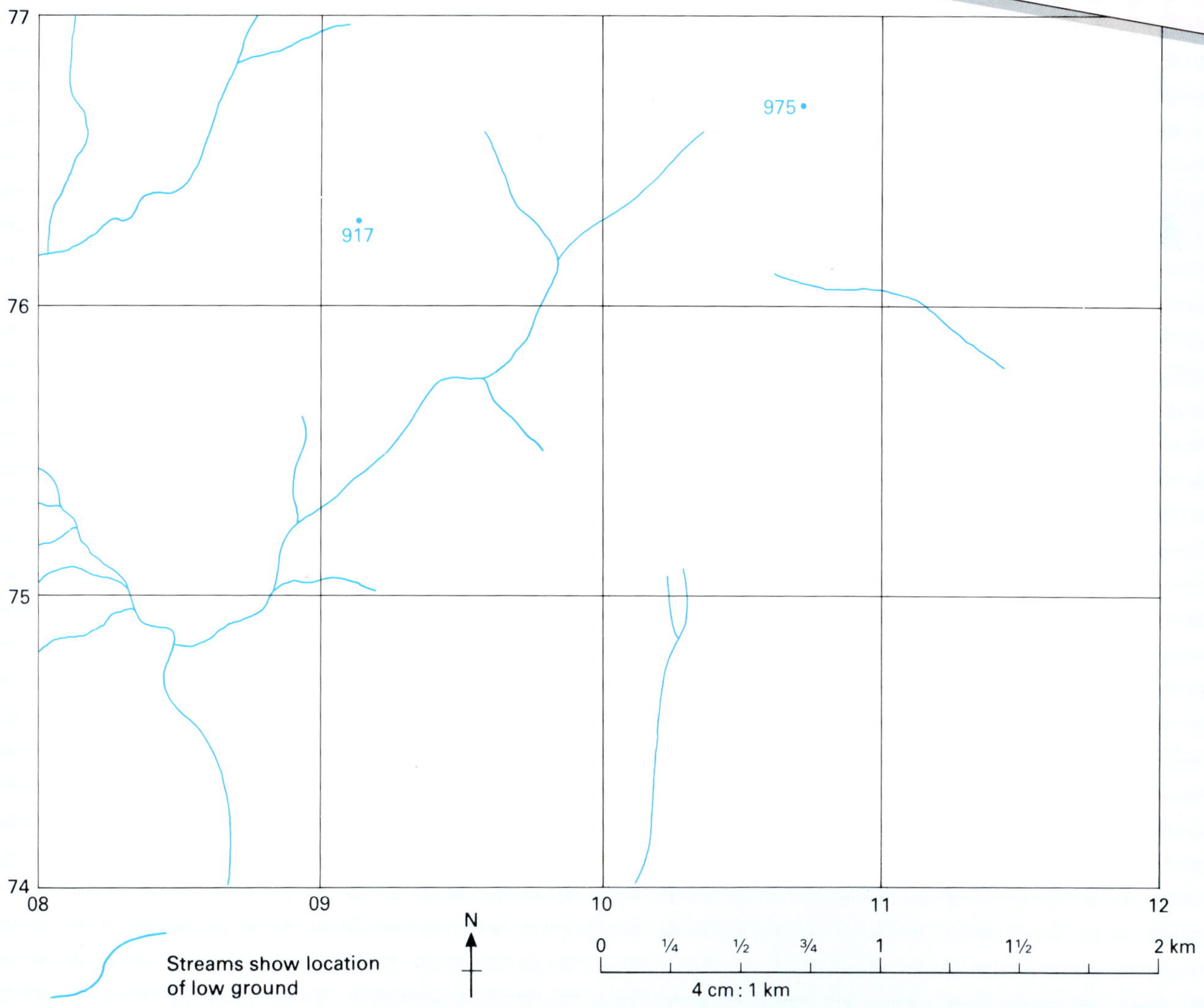

Streams show location of low ground

N

0   ¼   ½   ¾   1   1½   2 km

4 cm : 1 km

10 MAPSKILLS

ASSIGNMENT 10: Oxfordshire
Calculating area

The grid squares on an OS map can be used to work out the area of any large feature. Each grid square on a 1:50 000 or 1:25 000 map is 1km X 1km. This means that the grid square has a total area of 1 km².

Say you want to calculate the area of the lake shown in the diagram.

- Work out how many full squares are covered by the lake (each one is 1 km²)
- For the squares which are only partly covered by the lake estimate whether they are ¼, ½ or ¾ covered

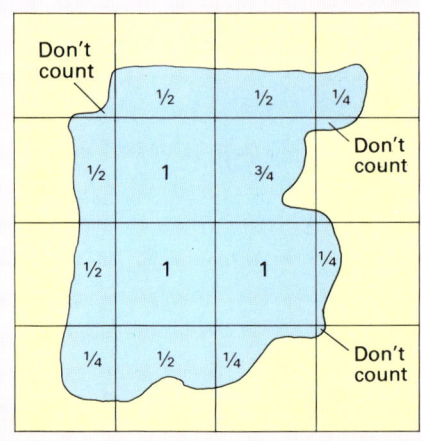

- Add up the total to give a reasonable estimate of the area of the lake, which is:

3 full squares = 3 km²
1 × ¾ square = ¾ km²
5 × ½ squares = 2½ km²
4 × ¼ squares = 1 km²

Total = 7¼ km²

Map enlargement and reduction

The map grid also helps when we need to draw a larger or smaller scale version of a map (map enlargement and reduction.)

The diagram below shows what a *half-scale* map would look like. These are the steps to follow:

1 First draw a grid of the size that you need, (in this example the grid is simply drawn at half the size).
2 Locate any obvious *point features*, such as buildings or hill tops. You can do this accurately using six-figure map references, as they will be the same on grids of any size.
3 Mark on the main *line features*, such as roads and rivers. Do this by noting where line features cross grid lines.
4 Finally, *remember to add the correct scale* to the map you have drawn.

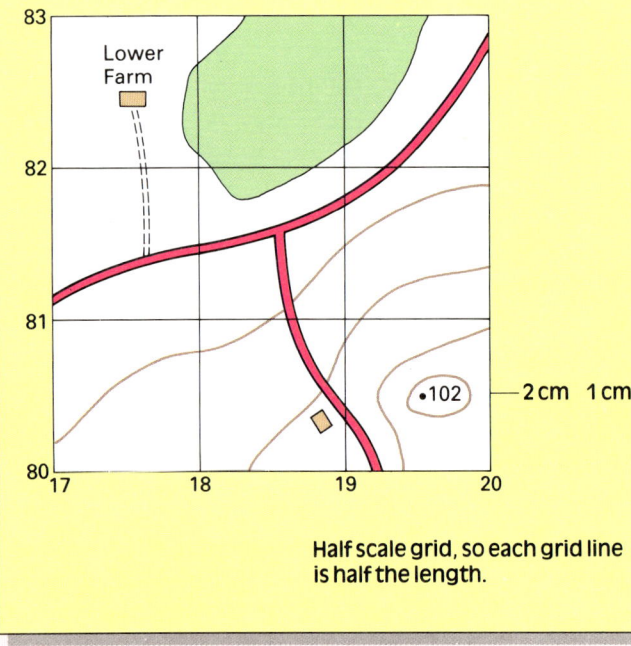

Half scale grid, so each grid line is half the length.

Test your skill 1

1 **Shabbington** and **Waterperry Woods** are the largest woods shown on the map opposite. What is the total area of these two woods combined?
2 Calculate the area of **Coniston Water** shown on the map on page 34.

Test your skill 2

1 Draw a map of the information in grid squares 5907, 6007, 5908, 6008 at a scale twice that of the map opposite.
2 The area shown on the map opposite is located on the north eastern edge of the city of Oxford.
  a Is the A40 main road single or dual carriageway?
  b Give a square reference for each of these features: a Country Park, a Nature Reserve, an Agricultural Centre
  c What makes Upper Arncott (6117) different from the other villages in the area?
3 In the area between grid lines 07 and 15 used to stand the ancient and great Forest of Bernwood. Today the remains of Bernwood can be seen in the many smaller woods. How many named woods are there in the area between those grid lines?
4 Find the area called **Otmoor**. In what ways is Otmoor different from the surrounding countryside? There are both human and physical points to make in your answer.

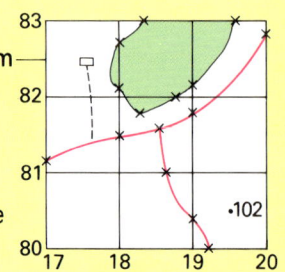

Crosses show some key points for transferring information onto half-scale map.

Don't try to put all the information onto a smaller map.

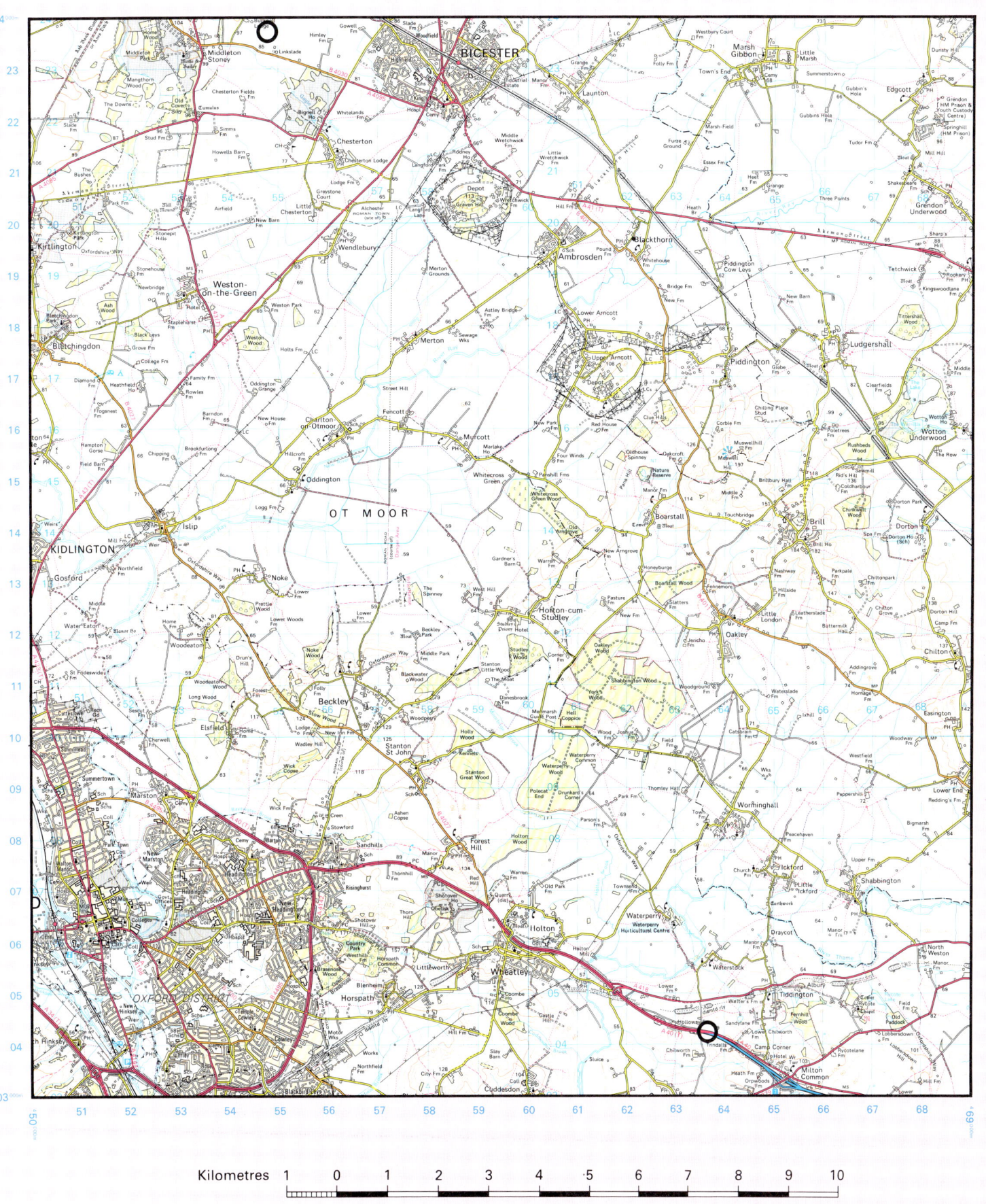

10 INVESTIGATION

Oxfordshire
Planning a motorway route

Briefing

The last long stretch of motorway which the government plans to build in Britain is the M40 between London and Birmingham. As the map shows, the London-Oxford section of the M40 is already built and in use.

A new motorway has a major impact on an area, and so planning and building a motorway always causes conflicts. Some people oppose the whole idea of building motorways. Other groups of people have strong views about where the route of a motorway should or should not go.

The section of the planned M40 which has caused most conflict is the part of the motorway which crosses the area of Oxfordshire shown on the map on the previous page. The map shows the two points that this section of motorway has to join. The question is which route should it take?

Your task is to investigate the conflicting views on the route, and to plan what you think would be the best route.

Work programmes A, B and C

Work either on your own or with somebody else. If you work in a pair, you can discuss ideas, but you should both carry out all the tasks involved.

Report back

Your final investigation report will include written comments and a carefully drawn tracing overlay map.

A: What are people's views?

The views of some of the people who have spoken at the Public Inquiry are outlined on the opposite page. Read through their comments carefully.

What are the points those people make about the motorway route? Make notes which summarise the main points made.

Now look at the map on the previous page, which shows the area the motorway will have to cross. Think about how the points you have noted might affect the route the M40 could take.

B: Planning a route

Place a sheet of tracing paper over the map on the previous page. On your tracing overlay:

- Draw on a map grid
- Mark the two points which the motorway has to join

Plan some possible routes for the motorway across this area. Work in pencil at this stage. Take account of your own and other peoples' ideas about routes.

Which route do you think would be the best? When you have decided, mark the route in colour on your overlay.

C: Comparing routes

The so-called 'preferred route', the one that the Department of the Environment favours, is shown on the map on page 48.

By transferring that information onto your own tracing overlay, show where the DoE's preferred route crosses the area.

How does the DoE route compare with yours? Compare and analyse the two routes in as much detail as you can.

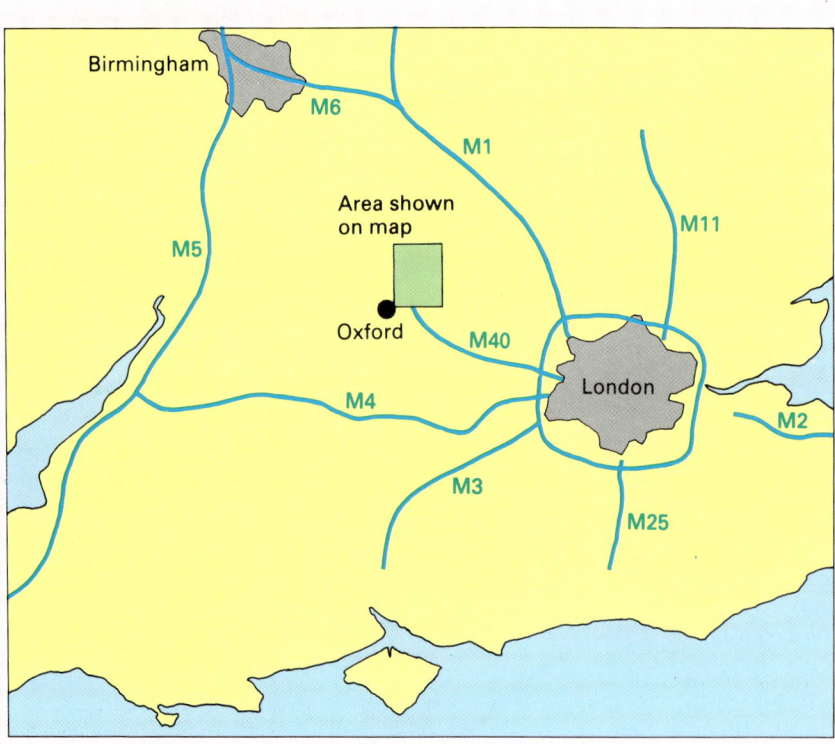

'It would be an environmental disaster if the motorway crosses Otmoor. Otmoor is unique – an area of unspoiled and unchanged natural beauty, there's nothing else like it in SE England. Putting the motorway across Otmoor would be an act of vandalism.'

GLOOM OR DELIGHT?

Motorway route to be announced

The decision on the route of the Oxfordshire section of the M40 will be announced in the New Year, according to a press release from the Department of the Environment yesterday. By that time the Minister will have had time to study the report of his Inspector, who carried out the long-running Public Inquiry. Meanwhile pro- and anti-motorway groups continue to argue their cases.

'I don't think we need a motorway at all. This is good farmland. Build a damn great motorway over it and it will be lost to farming for ever. Building motorways only encourages more vehicles in the roads.'

'The sooner the motorway is built the better. Business would benefit, and Oxfordshire as a whole would benefit. You can't stop progress, so let's stop sitting around discussing it. What we need is the shortest and most direct route, the one that will be quickest and cheapest to build.'

'Traffic on the existing A40 around Oxford is already horrendous. If we not careful the motorway could make that worse. If the motorway route passed as close to Oxford as possible, it would take traffic away from the existing A40, and Oxfordshire really would benefit.'

'We have got to think about the cost. It costs about £2 million to build a kilometre of motorway – that's a lot of money. We owe it to the taxpayer to make the route as short and direct as possible, but at the same time trying to preserve things that really are important.'

'Yes, and Waterperry Wood is a butterfly sanctuary. There are some rare and protected species there.'

'Preserving the ancient woodlands must be the main concern. Shabbington, Waterperry, Holton, Stanton Great Wood have been there for centuries. They are all that remain of Bernwood Forest. There are deer, foxes, badgers, owls and many other animals in those woods. The motorway could easily destroy their habitat.'

'This is a beautiful country area. The people who live in the villages around here don't want a motorway near them. Most of them won't be using it anyway. It's for heavy lorries going from London to Birmingham. If there is going to be a motorway it should stay away from peoples' homes.'

Key to 1:50 000 map extracts

ROADS AND PATHS
Not necessarily rights of way

VOIES DE COMMUNICATIONS
VERKEHRSNETZ

Service area M40, Junction number 7, Elevated, En Viaduc, überhöht	Motorway (dual carriageway)	Autoroute (chaussées separées) avec aire de service et échangeur avec numero de l'échangeur	Autobahn (zweibahnig) mit Versorgungs- und Anschlussstelle sowie Nummer der Anschlussstelle
	Motorway under construction	Autoroute en construction	Autobahn im Bau
Unfenced / Footbridge / A 34 (T) / Sans clôture / Passerelle Fussgängerbrücke	Trunk road	Route de grande circulation	Fernverkehrsstrasse
Dual carriageway A 415 / Chaussées separées / Zweibahnig	Main road	Route principale	Hauptstrasse
	Main road under construction	Route principale en construction	Hauptstrasse im Bau
Uneingehegt B 4011	Secondary road	Route secondaire	Nebenstrasse
A 855 / B 885	Narrow road with passing places	Route étroite avec voies de dépassement	Enge Strasse mit Ausweich-Überholstellen
Bridge / Pont / Brücke	Road generally more than 4 m wide	Route généralement de plus de 4 m de largeur	Strasse, Minimalbreite im allg. 4 m
	Road generally less than 4 m wide	Route généralement de moins de 4 m de largeur	Strasse, Maximalbreite im allg. 4 m
	Other road, drive or track	Autre route, allée ou sentier	Sonstige Strasse, Zufahrt, oder Feldweg
	Path	Sentier	Fussweg
	Gradient: 1 in 5 and steeper / 1 in 7 to 1 in 5	Pente: 20% et plus / de 14% à 20%	Steigungen: 20% und mehr / 14% bis 20%
	Gates / Road tunnel	Barrières / Tunnel routier	Schranken / Strassentunnel
Ferry P / Ferry V	Ferry (passenger) / Ferry (vehicle)	Bac pour piétons / Bac pour véhicules	Personenfähre / Autofähre

ABBREVIATIONS

P	Post office	CH	Clubhouse
PH	Public house	PC	Public convenience (in rural areas)
MS	Milestone	TH	Town Hall, Guildhall or equivalent
MP	Milepost	CG	Coastguard

ANTIQUITIES

VILLA Roman ⚔ Battlefield (with date) + Position of antiquity which cannot be drawn to scale
Castle Non-Roman ☆ Tumulus

𝔐 Ancient Monuments and Historic Buildings in the care of the Secretaries of State for the Environment, for Scotland and for Wales and that are open to the public

The revision date of archaeological information varies over the sheet

HEIGHTS

Contours are at 10 metres vertical interval

•144 Heights are to the nearest metre above mean sea level

ROCK FEATURES

outcrop, cliff, scree

Heights shown close to a triangulation pillar refer to the station height at ground level and not necessarily to the summit.

GENERAL FEATURES

- Electricity transmission line (with pylons spaced conventionally)
- Pipe line (arrow indicates direction of flow)
- Buildings (ruin)
- Public buildings (selected)
- Bus or coach station
- Coniferous wood
- Non-coniferous wood
- Mixed wood
- Orchard
- Park or ornamental grounds
- Quarry
- Spoil heap, refuse tip or dump
- Radio or TV mast
- Church or Chapel { with tower / with spire / without tower or spire }
- Chimney or tower
- Glasshouse
- Graticule intersection at 5' intervals
- Heliport
- Triangulation pillar
- Windmill with or without sails
- Windpump

PUBLIC RIGHTS OF WAY
(Not applicable to Scotland)

- Footpath
- Bridleway
- Road used as a public path
- Byway open to all traffic
- Danger Area — MOD Ranges in the area. Danger. Observe warning notices

BOUNDARIES

- National
- County, Region or Islands Area
- London Borough
- District
- National Park or Forest Park
- NT National Trust — NT always open / NT opening restricted
- FC Forestry Commission — Pedestrians only - observe local signs

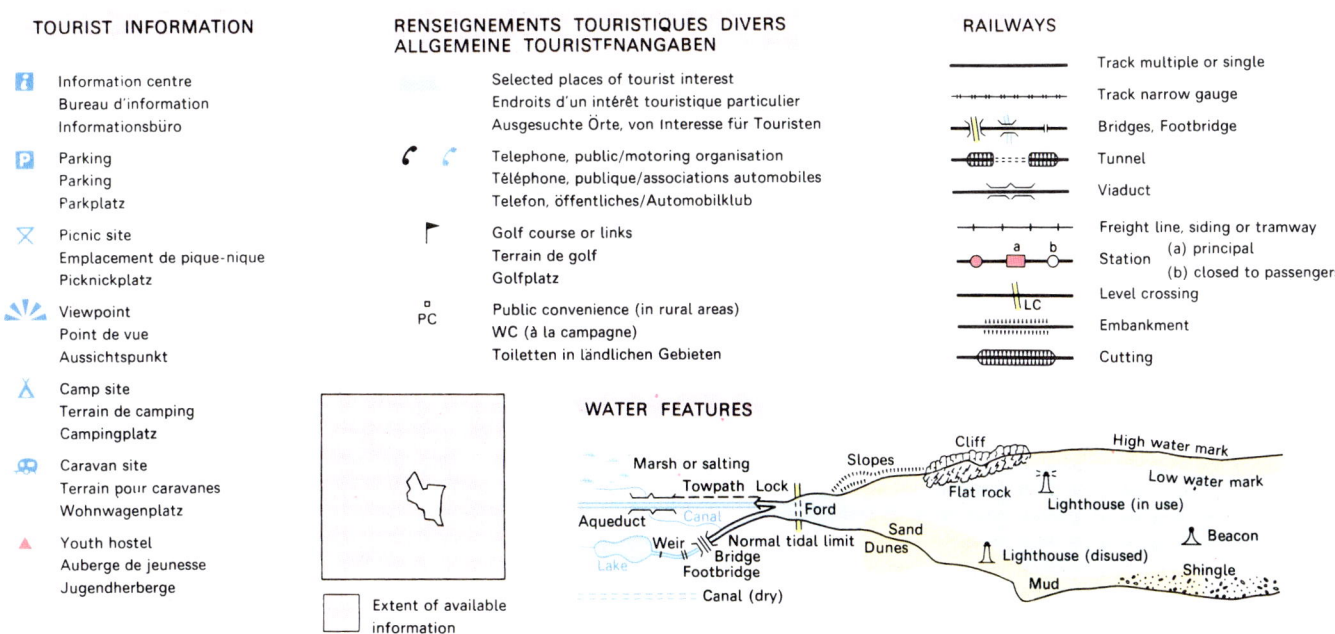

Key to 1:25 000 map extracts

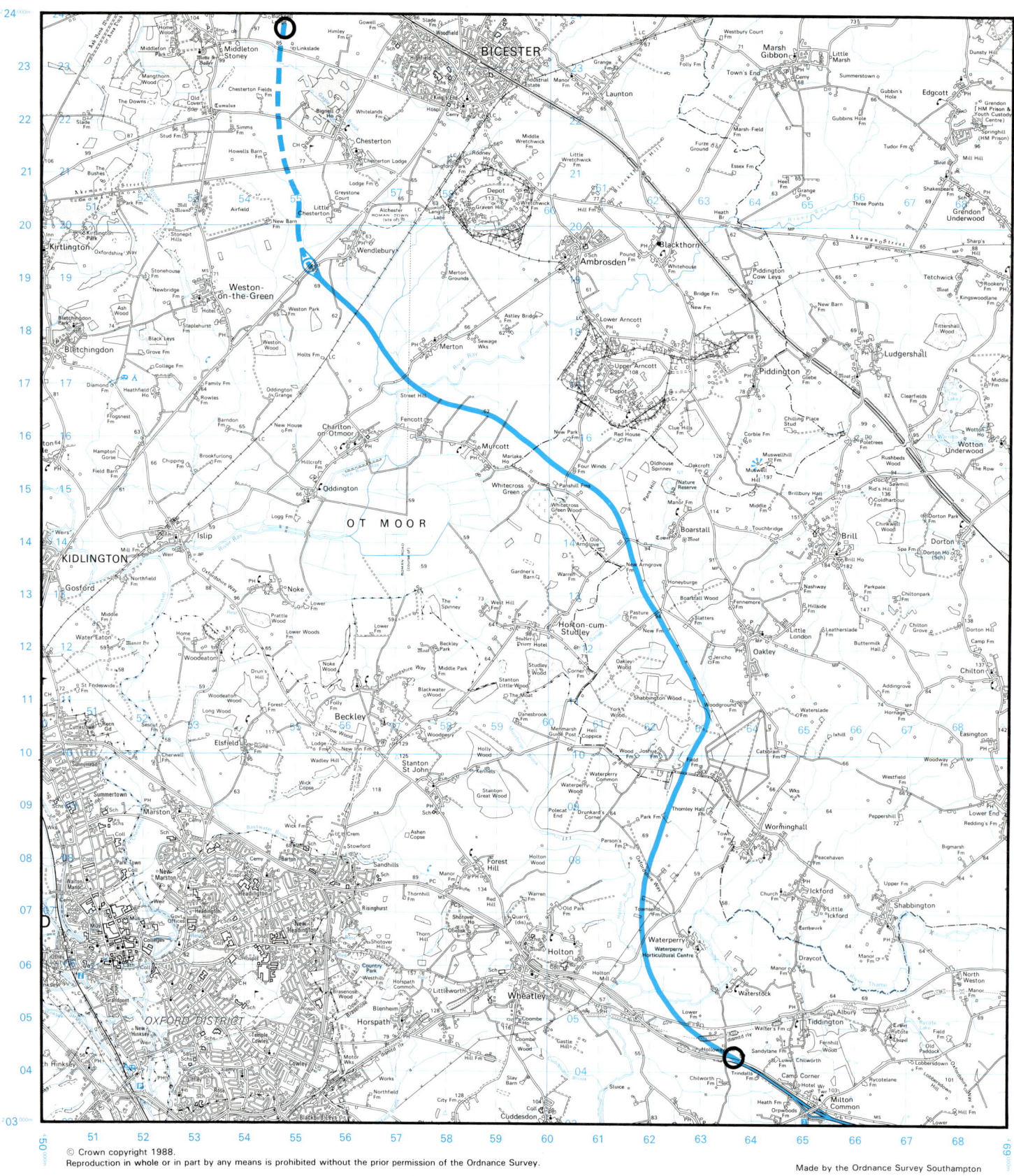